**African sculpture
an anthology**

D1247868

Designed by Gillian Greenwood

William Fagg and Margaret Plass

AFRICAN

SCULPTURE
an anthology

studio vista | dutton pictureback
General editor David Herbert

Sources of photographs

Allison, Philip 18, 19
Bradbury, R. E. 123
British Museum 8a, 33b, 35, 63, 67, 68, 80a, 87, 102b, 139, 148, 149, 150a, 158
Burney, S. 113
Elisofon, Eliot 30, 47–49, 54, 70, 75, 88, 119, 133, 137, 145, 146a
Etnografisch Museum, Antwerp 81
Fagg, Bernard 8b, 32
Institute of Arts, Detroit 118
Linden-Museum, Stuttgart 14, 16, 40a
Little, Lisa 33a
Musée Royal de l'Afrique Centrale, Tervuren 38, 50a, 82a
Newman, Arnold 13, 155
Nigerian Museum, Lagos 10, 143
Parade Studios Inc, Cleveland, Ohio 66
Ratton, Charles 78b, 97a, 100, 105, 111, 136, 150b
Städtische Sammlungen für Kunst- und Kulturgeschichte, Ulm 112, 114
Städtisches Museum für Völkerkunde, Frankfurt 102a
Uht, Charles 84
University Museum, Philadelphia 31b, 36, 85, 115, 129, 131a, b
Virginia Museum of Fine Arts, Richmond 142
Ward Price, H. L. 60
Willett, Frank 20
All other photographs are by William Fagg

© Studio Vista Limited 1964
Reprinted 1966, 1968
Published in London by Studio Vista Limited
and in New York by E. P. Dutton and Co Inc
201 Park Avenue South, New York, NY 10003
Distributed in Canada by General Publishing Co Limited
30 Lesmill Road, Don Mills, Toronto, Ontario
Set in 8pt Univers, 2pts leaded
Made and printed in Great Britain by
Richard Clay (The Chaucer Press), Ltd, Bungay, Suffolk
SBN 289.36804.9

Introduction

We have called our book an anthology not in order to distinguish it from other books on African art—for indeed they are all somewhat of this character—but rather to draw the reader's attention to the personal character of our selection, as well as to the experimental nature of the book. Having been often irritated by the tendency of previous writers to cannibalize earlier books, thus rendering many fine sculptures hackneyed by excessive repetition, we have almost completely avoided works which have been previously published in book form (unless long out of print). (This is by no means difficult, and material for ten such books could be found, without repetition, in the British Museum collections alone.) Such being our intention, this is not to be regarded as our entry for the 200 Greatest Masterpieces of African Sculpture; we do not see any reason to put that kind of selection on public record.

Our purpose is rather to try what is, for us at least, a new way of looking at African art, which we hope may be helpful to the wide public, probably unfamiliar with it but having some general interest in art, to whom the book is addressed. As ethnologists interested in art history, we are well aware that many of the styles and movements widely supposed to have developed for the first time in Europe—even 'Art Nouveau'—really represent recurrent modes in the human arts, modes which have always been available to the artist, within the limits of his human and natural environment. So it occurred to us that it would be interesting, and might be illuminating, to examine some African sculptures in relation to some of these European concepts of art and to see how far, if at all, they are applicable. Since these categories are those in which we are accustomed to think about the more familiar kinds of art, the attempt to use them in the very different conditions of African art may help us to free ourselves from the preconceptions which we unconsciously harbour about the exotic arts. So we have chosen, from among the pieces readily available to us in the British Museum, the University Museum of Philadelphia and various other museum and private collections, those which seemed most relevant to our purpose, the identification of different types of sculptural form in African art. For our book is above all about form—though we insist that form cannot be understood without reference to its cultural matrix. We hope for the indulgence of those who are more expert than we in the history of European art and who may find that we have sometimes gone astray in our understanding of the concepts of their chosen fields of study.

5

At the same time we have tried to confine our choice so far as possible to pieces which are artistically pleasing, and any reader who does not wish to be encumbered with our attempted correlations of European and African modes is welcome to use our book as a 'museum without walls', in which the works have been 'hung' in what we intend to be artistic sympathy with each other, and not according to the more usual geographical–ethnographical order. (All the same, we would point out that the classification of sculptural forms is itself a part—if a neglected one—of ethnology.) Those who regret the dispersal of objects from one tribe or area will find them gathered together again (by page numbers) in the list of tribes accompanying the map on page 159.

Since African art is the product of an environment so different from the one which we know and take for granted when we evaluate European art, a few general observations about it may be helpful to the reader. In the first place, traditional sculpture— and we are not concerned here with 'contemporary' African art, which for all its merits is an extension of European art by a kind of voluntary cultural colonialism—is almost confined to the great basins of the Niger and Congo Rivers, that is to say to an area bounded on the north and south by the Sahara and Kalahari Deserts and on the east and west by the Great Lakes and the Atlantic Ocean. This area is vast enough, but a vaster area still is almost devoid of sculpture, and it cannot be said that the several explanations which have been offered for this great dichotomy are altogether satisfying, even when taken together. Certainly it cannot be merely a matter of geographical environment, for the art area itself includes most types of habitat, and sculpture has flourished alike in the humid creeks and mangrove swamps of the Niger Delta, in the primeval rain forest of the Congo, in the rolling grasslands of the Cameroons and central Nigeria, and in the craggy escarpments and barren scrub of the Sahel, the Sahara fringe. If we compare man's activities east and west of the Lakes, we find that most Niger–Congo tribes are settled agriculturalists who have been there for thousands of years, whereas the pastoral tribes are mostly in East and North-East Africa; great movements of peoples in the wide East African corridor have been compounded by the incidence of Islamic iconoclasm all along the coast and often far into the interior. These facts may be a partial explanation for the artistic poverty of the East and South, yet we should still expect to find far more sculpture than we do among the many agriculturalists who co-exist with the East African nomads—and the nomads of Central Asia produced some of the finest of all tribal art.

We hope that this book will serve to display convincingly the immense variety of African sculptural forms. To a casual glance indeed it may suggest a chaotic confusion of unrestrained stylistic inventiveness such as that which obtains in the art of the Western world today. But African art is no product of romantic decadence; its image, when properly understood, is rather that of a disciplined yet flexible classicism. The apparent confusion arises simply from the fact that the art of each tribe is a separate universe; in traditional Africa the language of art is not intertribal, as the language of Western art is international. When we examine the art of a single tribe we find it to be an entity as coherent and consistent as the tribal religion and philosophy which largely inspired it. Art, in fact, like language, religion, social institutions and customary law, is one of the ways in which a tribe (by its nature an 'in-group') distinguishes itself from its neighbours. In Africa, then, art does know frontiers, and tribality is of its essence.

In the perspective of history, when today's propaganda pamphlets have been blown away by further winds of change, it will doubtless be seen that the most important and significant contribution made to Africa by the colonial system was the political movements, at present usually called 'nationalism', which helped to bring about its dissolution, and whose forms are largely traceable to the patterns established by the European Socialist revolutions of 1848. Somewhat similarly, the supposititious philosophy of *négritude*, which is still being actively canvassed in some quarters, is a product of Parisian existentialism and has no roots in Africa, for which reason we should prefer to call it *blanchitude*. Again, 'African contemporary art' is in large part merely a demonstration that Africans—who are no less well endowed with artistic genius and intelligence than people of other races—are quite capable of working in the international or Western style of art, and here again African roots are rarely discernible—not surprisingly, since their patrons are still almost exclusively European and American. In these and many other ways the people of Africa are under heavy but largely subliminal pressure to give up their birthright for a mess of pottage.

Rarely in human history can a people have been confronted with an overt and conscious choice between having an art of their own—their greatest contribution to the richness of human culture —and adopting one from abroad, from a supposedly 'higher' civilization. Yet this choice does confront hundreds of African peoples today, if only their statesmen and thinkers will give time to weighing it. We do not mean that contemporary art should be discouraged, or cease to be encouraged in those fitted for it. But we do believe that Africans are still largely unaware of the immense value of their tribal art to the world and of the danger that the African values which it represents may soon become fossilized in the world's museums.

You must see in nature
the cylinder, the sphere and the cone

Cézanne's best-known dictum is often quoted as a kind of summary charter of the modern movement in art; and so it was. But we prefer to consider it here as the clearest explicit appreciation by the early modern artists of the nature of conceptual art, which is not modern but ancient. For people brought up under the influence of the Renaissance tradition, it is usually conceptual art—in which the artist seeks to communicate not the appearance of things but his own ideas or concepts about them—which seems to need explanation. But when we survey the whole field of man's artistic accomplishment, it is rather the Graeco-Romano-Renaissance specialization in naturalistic imitation which appears out of step with the rest of the world—even though the intensity of this specialization produced some of the greatest of all works of art.

We illustrate Cézanne's three specimen geometrical forms from two of the earliest phases of African sculpture—the ancient cultures of Nok and Ife. The Nok Culture—discovered by Bernard Fagg in 1943 in the tin mines of Northern Nigeria—flourished in the last few hundred years before Christ, at the very beginning of the Iron Age, and so the terra-cottas which survive from it are by far the oldest African sculptures that we know of. Yet its forms are some of the boldest and most original in all African art, and varied enough to have provided the seeds of many of the diverse styles illustrated in this book. The cylinder head (8 *in*)—a kind of Mercator's Projection of the human head—the sphere ($3\frac{1}{2}$ *in*) and the inverted cone ($8\frac{1}{4}$ *in*) are all in the Jos Museum. The fourth terra-cotta, a reconciliation of the conical form with a subtle naturalism, is from ancient Ife and so is presumed to date from about the twelfth or thirteenth century AD (*c* 6 *in*).

Cone, sphere and cylinder all appear in this ancestor figure (*ekpu*) from the Oron clan of Calabar (about 36 *in*; registered as No. 341 in the Oron Museum); it is indeed a composition made up of these three elements. The Oron are nominally a clan of the Ibibio, but their style of carving, now extinct for half a century, was all their own. Several hundred *ekpu* carvings still exist, made by many hands over the past two centuries, and when seen in mass, as in the Oron Museum, they are among the most moving, in their sculptural expression of tribal belief, of all the forms of African art. The juxtaposition of almost dissociated geometrical forms reminds us of Brancusi, especially in his 'Adam and Eve' series; although he can never have seen an Oron carving, he was unsurpassed among modern artists in his profound understanding of the sculptural conceptions of tribal art. But of course the Oron carvers were free of the intellectualism which the modern artist cannot escape.

10

In a corner of the old Musée de la France d'Outremer in Paris, there could be seen this remarkable example of African simplification of form. It is a replica (made by Maillol's bronzefounder) of a mask from the Fang tribe of Gaboon and beneath it was this legend: *L'original avait été donné, en 1905, à Maurice de Vlaminck qui le vendit à Derain. Derain emporta le masque dans son atelier de la rue de Tourlaque, où Picasso et Matisse, en le voyant, furent troublés et remués. Ambroise Vollard demanda alors à Derain la permission de faire couler le masque en bronze. Ce bronze est donc le moulage de la première pièce d'art nègre qui ait influencé l'art contemporain et créé, en réaction contre l'Impressionisme, un courant stylistique d'où devaient sortir le Néo-primitivisme et le Cubisme. (Don de M. Lucien Vollard.) The wooden original is now in the Toledo (Ohio) Museum of Art.*

Let us, in the next few pages, examine a few more of the African conceptualizations—going beyond the three forms singled out by Cézanne, but still essentially of a simplifying character—which so 'troubled and moved' the early Post-Impressionists. On this page is one of the six recorded masks from the Nupe of Northern Nigeria—all of them collected by Leo Frobenius in Mokwa in 1910–11 (four in Germany, one in Basel). This, the best of the six, has only recently come to light and is now in the British Museum (Webster Plass collections, $25\frac{1}{2}$ *in*). The human face is here simplified as an ovoid form, surmounted by animal horns, not very realistically carved, which echo the outline of the face itself. The Nupe were converted to Islam by force of arms in about 1830 when the great Fulani warrior Malam Dendo subdued the kingdom; apart from some relief carving on doors, these few masks are almost the sole evidence of the survival of representational art there.

12

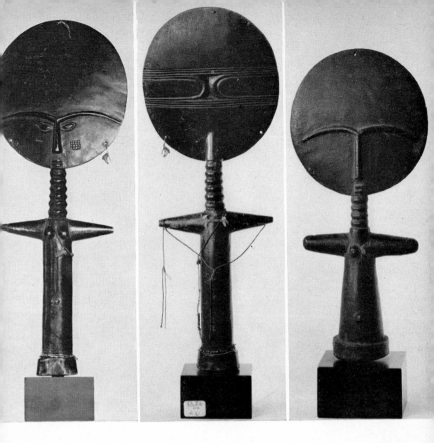

Art among the Ashanti of Ghana has been dominated for three centuries past by gold (see pages 115–117), and representational carving is almost confined to the charming dolls (*akua 'ba*) carried by small girls. They are said to embody the Ashanti ideal of beauty, the head being conceived, or conceptualized, as a lens-shaped disc set at a slight backward tilt on a cylindrical body; a less realistic representation of a human head can hardly be imagined, yet one sees in Ashanti, as among no other African people, a proportion of children (notably in the royal families) whose high, wide foreheads do at once remind one of the *akua 'ba*. However, the flatness of the carved heads may be partly because their owners tuck them into their waist-cloths at the small of the back, like real babies. These two (centre is back view of left) are in the collection of Mr Arnold Newman of New York (14$\frac{1}{4}$ and 9 *in*).

13

There are hundreds of different ways of carving an elephant in African art, most of them conceived as here by way of simplification, some by way of elaboration as on page 117, but often far less easily recognizable than in this Baluba stool in the Linden-Museum at Stuttgart (*c* 10 *in*). The great flaring legs express the stability at once of the elephant and of the stool.

We have mentioned Brancusi, and he would surely have recognized a kindred spirit in the carver of this faceless doll (7 *in*) collected for the British Museum in 1909 by Torday at Mushenge, the royal capital of the Bakuba tribe between the Kasai and Sankuru Rivers in the Congo. The child who played with this would learn by a kind of osmosis the concept of head form which is peculiar to the Bakuba artists, and especially to those eminent carvers-in-ordinary—one in each reign—whose duty it was to carve the famous portrait statues of the kings.

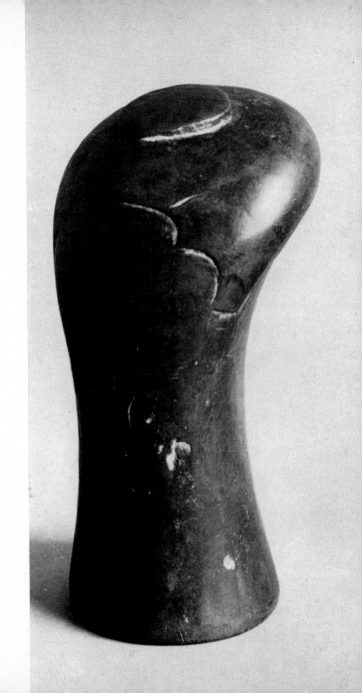

James Thurber writes in one of his essays of his Negro house-
maid who called his (early-type) refrigerator 'the doom-shaped
thing', and here we see how in two widely separated parts of
West Africa—among the Senufo of the northern Ivory Coast and
the Chamba of Northern Nigeria near the Cameroons border—
the concept of a high dome has been used to give a more than
usually awesome effect to types of mask which normally rely on
a more horizontal line. The Chamba example, left, was collected
over fifty years ago by Frobenius and appears to represent a bush
cow (Linden-Museum, Stuttgart, length 24 *in*; a side view has
been published in von Sydow, *Afrikanische Plastik,* 1954, plate
120c). The Senufo carving above, though not among the finest of
its kind, shows originality in the strong emphasis on the dome-like
form dominating the whole (British Museum, length $31\frac{1}{2}$ *in*).

African sculptors are usually very sensitive to the qualities of their raw materials, and completely different styles are commonly in use in the same tribe for brass-casting and for woodcarving. As this book illustrates, woodcarving predominates overwhelmingly as the main medium for sculpture in Africa, though ivory is also worked by much the same techniques among most of the West African tribes. Stone has never been widely used there either in architecture or in sculpture, perhaps because of a positive preference for the ephemeral—the mud house and the termite-prone woodcarving. In all the great area of the Niger and Congo basins (in which almost all African plastic art was concentrated), stone-carving seems to have been practised only in four places, though suitable stone is much more generally available: in Sierra Leone and the neighbouring Kissi area of Guinea; around Ife in Western Nigeria; on the upper Cross River near the Cameroons border of Eastern Nigeria; and on the south bank of the Congo where the Kingdom of Kongo once flourished. In all but the third of these, soapstone or steatite—the most easily worked of stones—was much used, though at Ife quartz and granite were used for the more im-

portant works. This may provide us with a clue to the attitude of the West African artists to the use of stone, for it suggests that they tended to regard it less as a material in its own right, with its own artistic conceptions of form, than as a kind of extension of the normal range of materials available to the 'subtractive' artist— by which we mean one who forms a work by the cutting-away of material from a block (as opposed to the 'additive' artist, who forms it by adding more material such as clay or wax).

We illustrate on these two pages some of nearly 300 stone figures which have been recently recorded for the Nigerian Department of Antiquities by Mr Philip Allison in the Ekoi country around Ikom on the upper Cross River. They were carved, probably over several hundred years up to about 1900, as memorials to dead clan heads. The carving is nearer to the engraver's than to the sculptor's art, and little shaping seems to have been applied to the naturally more or less cylindrical boulders. So the usual opinion that they are phallic in character may be unnecessary as an explanation of their form, which could be interpreted as a demonstration of a healthy respect for hard basalt.

Only in the ancient culture of Ife in central Yorubaland—perhaps about AD 1300—do we find evidence of real and conscious virtuosity in the working of stone: the Ife masons made the largest monoliths (such as the nineteen-foot 'staff of Oranmiyan'), carved perversely elaborate ritual stools out of great blocks of intractable quartz, and also sculptured human and animal figures in semi-naturalistic form, such as the one seen above, which bears some resemblance to an achondroplasic dwarf. It is said to represent one Ore and stood, about two and a half feet high, at the end of a long grove (called Igbo Ore) just outside the town of Ife; (Ife Museum; $31\frac{1}{2}$ *in* high).

Where only soft stone is used, such as the rather greasy soapstone (easily carved with a small knife, yet not friable), the sculptures usually have a much less 'stony' look and their forms are often just as appropriate to wood. Opposite are two old figures (British Museum, $8\frac{1}{2}$ and 10 *in* high) from the Kissi country of Sierra Leone near the border of Guinea. (The Kissi style is also remarkable for the occurrence of the 'archaic smile', though, as in ancient Greece and Central America, it is doubtful whether a smile is what the artists had in mind.)

The strong vertical axis of the Kissi stonecarvings (which are called *pomdo*, pl. *pomtan*) is quite different from the design of the better-known *nomoli* figures are found in the soil over large parts of Sierra Leone; in these the dominant axes are rather in the horizontal direction, powerful head and limb forms being projected (sometimes cantilevered) forward as in this piece (British Museum, $7\frac{1}{4}$ *in*). It now seems certain that these soapstone *nomoli* were being made during the sixteenth century by the ancestors of the present Sherbro and possibly Temne tribes, who in those days occupied large areas of the country from which the Mande-Fu-speaking Mende later drove them. The identity of style (and some striking details of subject matter) between the *nomoli* and the majority of the Afro-Portuguese ivory saltcellars, spoons and hunting horns which appeared in European collections at that time is supported by the praise given by contemporary Portuguese travellers to the ivory-workers of Sherbro. And this identity also confirms our view that the *nomoli* forms lack stylistic qualities specially appropriate to stonecarving.

The massive pedestal heads found (much more rarely) in the same area (above, British Museum, length $10\frac{1}{2}$ *in*) illustrate the same point equally well. The nearest parallels to these curious backward-tilted faces are the wooden *Gelede* masks of the Yoruba of Nigeria and, even more distant, the masks of the southern Makonde of northern Mozambique near the East African coast; but close though the similarity of sculptural conception is, the possibility of any connection between them seems extremely remote.

We do not for a moment suggest that African stone sculptures are any the worse for their lack of stylistic differentiation from wood sculpture. The head above seems to us a particularly beautiful work. Rather we use them to illustrate obliquely the high concentration of the African artistic genius in the wood-carver's craft.

The largest single group of stone figures in Africa is the well-known collection of 800 or more, mostly in soapstone, in the bush near the village of Esie in northern Yorubaland. The number of different hands represented runs into the hundreds, many of them of only average ability, but some of them artists of the first class. They do not closely resemble any recent Yoruba woodcarving styles in the area (though some details of subject matter are consistent with a Yoruba origin), but it is still possible that they were made by the Nupe, now a few miles to the north, a few centuries ago, since we do not know what style or styles of sculpture they may have practised before they were forcibly converted to Islam in the early nineteenth century. To the several examples which have been published (*eg* William Fagg, *Nigerian Images*, plates 74–76), we add a small head with elaborate coiffure and cicatrization (at Esie; about 9 *in*). Once more we find no special qualities of style derived from the nature of the stone; on the contrary, nearly all the heads have been separated from their bodies, no doubt through weaknesses arising in the too deep cutting, whereas the same forms executed in wood would have been thoroughly sound.

Last among our examples of woodcarving style in stone are these two *mintadi* figures, again in soapstone, from a group of the Bakongo tribe who live just to the south of the Congo River on the border of Angola and the Congo. Some hundreds of these ancestor memorial figures exist; some are quite recent, others perhaps as much as five hundred years old. Their style is identical with that of many wooden ancestor figures from the area, and undoubtedly survives from the old Kingdom of Kongo, which was flourishing when the Portuguese first reached the mouth of the Congo. These two figures (British Museum, 16½ and 16 *in*) may be in the middle range of age.

African metal sculptures, unlike those in stone, rarely show any stylistic relation to the woodcarver's art, and wrought iron work is the most autonomous of all. On the left we show the fine abstract staffs, with forms perhaps derived from animal horns, which mark the spot, now abandoned in the bush, where the legendary Kisra originally founded the Bariba city of Bussa on the upper Niger in the sixth century, but the staffs, about four feet high, cannot be more than a few hundred years old. (This spot and the present site of the city are to be submerged before long by the Niger Dam.)

Wrought iron sculpture among the Yoruba is often of great beauty, especially in its bird forms, and is for the most part reserved for the most fundamental and pervasive of the Yoruba cults, that of Osanyin, the spirit or principle of 'medicine' or life force. The three opposite, about five feet high, are in the palace of the Arinjale of Ise in southern Ekiti, Nigeria.

26

The Yoruba brass-casters, like the blacksmiths, often achieved great freedom of form, and never more than in these iron staffs with cast-on brass figures photographed during a festival at a remote village in eastern Ilorin Province. A mass of them, about four and a half feet high, were stuck in the ground in front of a temporary shrine to the goddess of the festival, while her wooden figure was borne round in a processional dance on the head of a small girl.

Most Yoruba brass-casting is done by the lost-wax process, in which a wax model is translated into metal. But at Obo, where these staffs must have been made, the latex of the cactus-like *oro agogo* (*Euphorbia kamerunica*) is used instead to form the models.

The Ashanti were the miniaturists of West Africa. The little brass weights which they used to cast, by the lost-wax process, for weighing gold dust offer us an extraordinarily rich documentation of the ordinary life of the people in the nineteenth century. Their natural and unpretentious charm is perhaps hardly enough to qualify them as an important art form, though they sometimes show an admirable spatial freedom achieved with a few simple blobs and threads of wax. Occasionally one of these miniatures has a monumentality of proportion which seems to overcome the limitation of size, and this example in the Plass collection (British Museum, collected about 1900 by Sir Cecil Armitage; $2\frac{1}{2}$ in) remarkably suggests a large modern sculpture, perhaps in some public park. We are reminded both of Henry Moore's admittedly more reposeful family groups and of the vigorous movement of Jacques Lipchitz's later works.

This magnificently sculptural headdress for the long abandoned *ogbom* 'play' of the Bende Ibo (Nigerian Museum, 33 *in*; for the front view see Elisofon and Fagg, *The Sculpture of Africa*, fig. 181) is reproduced here to draw attention to the brilliantly ingenious device—unparalleled to our knowledge in Africa—which the artist has used to bring the upper head to life, especially when it is seen in motion. The upper part of the nose is undercut on both sides so that the hole thus pierced appears as a flashing eye from either side. Henry Moore had independently used the same idea in a stone head in 1930. In 1951 the Nigerian piece was lent to the exhibition of Traditional Art from the Colonies in London during the Festival of Britain, and he was greatly interested during a visit to it to see how the Ibo artist had used this method of 'opening up' the human head. This seems to have led him to re-explore his own idea of 1930, and it appeared not only in the 'King and Queen' of 1952 but in many of his major works throughout the 1950s.

30

We do not of course recommend that African sculptures be admired for their resemblance, superficial or not, to modern styles; yet the reader who is familiar with Henri Matisse's painted odalisques may be all the readier to appreciate these two sculptures from Sierra Leone, that on the right certainly and the other probably from the Temne (left, British Museum, $38\frac{1}{2}$ *in*; right, University Museum, Philadelphia, $22\frac{1}{2}$ *in*). Their lines are graceful in a way which is extremely rare in African sculpture—noticeably different for example from the style of the neighbouring Mende, though that too is often very graceful in its own way. Our knowledge is not sufficient to tell us whether the booted woman at the left was intended by her creator to be also comical.

The twentieth century has been a great one for the naming of styles
in art, most of the names ending in '-ism'. But our century did not
invent most of these styles, any more than Linnaeus created flora
and fauna. Rather they are to be regarded as modes which have
always been available to the conceptual artist (much as the
classical or neo-classical architect draws at will on the Doric,
the Ionic or the Corinthian order), and which have been placed
at the disposal of Europe once more by the liberating effects of
the modernist revolution. No sooner had Cézanne's remark about
the cylinder, the sphere and the cone been published posthum-
ously than the basic natural form which he had forgotten was
recognized in a big way by the birth, or rather the rebirth, of

cubism; for whatever we may think of the transmigration of souls, the transmigration of art forms seems to be a fact of human history, even before the conscious eclecticism of our time.

In the next few pages we shall illustrate the frequent use of the cubist mode by African artists; and once again we can begin with the earliest known phase of African sculpture, the Nok culture of Northern Nigeria. The terra-cotta head opposite (Jos Museum, $5\frac{1}{2}$ in) was excavated nearly thirty feet deep in the tin mine near the village of Nok, after which this widespread culture is named.

On this page are two more recent examples of cubist wood-carving, from the Montol of Northern Nigeria (carved about 1952, collected and owned by Professor Roy Sieber; 12 in) and from the Isoko on the north-western edge of the Niger Delta (British Museum, 13 in). The principal tool of the African wood sculptor is the adze (which combines the functions of the European mallet and chisel), and it is easy to see how its use may favour the cubist variety of conceptualization.

Cubism is especially prevalent in the art of the Niger Delta tribes, and above all in that of the Ijo. This carving, called *ejiri*, is from the western Ijo, and is not for the cult of a god, spirit or ancestor, but is rather an impersonal machine for the control of the life force, and for its direction towards particular ends such as success in war or the recovery of lost goods. Its essential part is the massive quadruped which is variously said to be an elephant or a leopard and may combine features of both. Surmounting this monster is a human figure representing the owner of the *ejiri*. Similar carvings among their neighbours the Edo-speaking Urhobo and Isoko are called *ivbri*, and one such is represented on the head of the Isoko figure on page 33.

Among the tribes of the great basin of the Congo, the Basonge have especially favoured the

34

cubist mode in art, and their
fetishes perform a rather similar
function to that of the Ijo *ejiri*.
This word 'fetish' (from Portuguese *feitiço*) should not be
applied indiscriminately to
African art in general, including
carvings for the divine and
ancestral cults, but should be
reserved for impersonal 'machines' such as this massive
figure, 'made up' (as fetish means
in Portuguese) by the addition of
various materials or 'medicines'
drawn from the animal, vegetable
and mineral kingdoms, in order
to draw upon the immanent life
force of these substances; the
witch-doctor activates the fetish
by adding these medicines
(which may be secreted in the
cow horn) while performing appropriate ceremonies and incan-
tations. This great figure (40 *in*)
is in the British Museum.
Sculpturally, these Basonge
figures often show an affinity
with Polynesian carvings.

35

The brass-plated, low-relief funerary figures of the Bakota, who live near the Gaboon borders to the north of the Congo River, were placed in the baskets of ancestral bones on the family shrines to keep away evil influences. Although they played a great part in the development of European cubism—Picasso's series of *Danseuses d'Avignon* of 1907 being directly derived from them, with a dash of asymmetry—few of the sculptures themselves seem particularly good examples of the cubist mode (except for the type illustrated, by a piece from the Plass collection, in Elisofon and Fagg, fig. 224). The extremely rare unplated round sculpture which we illustrate (University Museum, Philadelphia, $22\frac{1}{2}$ *in*) does have a suggestion of the characteristic fragmentation of the subject matter into more or less triangular and lozenge-shaped intersecting facets. These figures, which are among the most stylized in African art, are apparently not representations of the ancestors, but impersonal protective charms.

36

Another tribe whose sculptures occasionally follow the cubist mode is the Balega (who used to be known by the Swahili form of the word, Warega) of the north-east Congo. They were until recently among the least-known of African peoples, even though their art has been greatly admired and collected (and also faked) in Europe and America for the past thirty years. They will shortly become one of the most thoroughly known, when Professor Daniel Biebuyck's exceptionally profound research among them during the 1950s is published. They are a small tribe, sparsely scattered over a large area, without towns or villages, political organization or chiefs, and united chiefly by the all-pervading *Bwami* association. This woodcarving in the Smithsonian Institution in Washington, D.C. (*c* 10 *in*) is (Professor Biebuyck tells us) of a type carried in the dance by members of the second highest level of the *Bwami*, and the arrangement of the cubist faces has reference to the practice of dancing with a mask attached to each shoulder.

This Balega wooden figure is from the great collection made by Professor Biebuyck for the Musée Royal de l'Afrique Centrale at Tervuren near Brussels (*c 6 in*). Such statues are emblems of rank held individually by members of the highest grade of the *Bwami* and are also used in initiations into this grade. This particular piece, with its curious cubistic body, was attached by raphia to the ceiling of the initiation hut and was hanging with the head downward. This proverb was sung about it: 'The bat hangs with head downward because of the bad words which it was told by the sun.'

38

The art of the smaller coastal tribes of Ghana is strongly influenced by that of the great Ashanti tribe to the north of them, but is often more highly stylized, as in this monumental stool supported on two Atlas-like figures, which was collected by J. Austin Freeman when serving on the boundary commission between the Gold Coast and Ivory Coast in the 1880s. It comes from Elmina, where a great Portuguese castle still marks its ancient status as a port for the gold and slave trades, and is now in the British Museum (width 28 *in*). Once more it is conceived in a form, rather different from the others which we have illustrated, of the cubist mode. From its exceptional size this would certainly have been the stool of a chief or king of the Fanti, the repository of a part of his soul.

Headrests are used in the Congo to protect the elaborate coiffures of their owners from contact with the ground while sleeping; many of them are supported on caryatid figures which, perhaps because of the heavy weight which they are to support, sometimes tend to take cubist forms. At left is one from the Bateke near Brazzaville (Linden-Museum, Stuttgart, *c* 5 *in*), and at right one which may be from the Batetela of the eastern Congo (collected by E. Torday in 1907–8, but not fully documented; British Museum, $5\frac{1}{2}$ *in*).

In European cubism the breaking-up of rounded natural forms into sharply intersecting facets or planes embodied a kind of 'synoptic vision', as though each form were being viewed from two (or more) points at once; it is most unlikely that this somewhat intellectual and self-conscious concept was present, consciously or unconsciously, in the minds of the African practitioners of the cubist mode. Synthesis rather than analysis or fragmentation seems to have been their object.

Our final example of African cubism—though traces of it can also be seen in other parts of this book—is taken from the Ibo of Eastern Nigeria (Talbot collection, British Museum, $6\frac{1}{2}$ *in*); for all its small size, it is one of the most monumental sculptures that we know.

The techniques of fragmentation of the image which are so characteristic of European cubism seem to have been inspired at least in part by a sort of revolutionary nihilism, a *Weltvernichtungsidee*. This is certainly the last thing which any tribal artist could have had in mind, and this should be a reminder to us that if we find convergences of form, however striking, between tribal and modern art, we must not assume any identity of purpose, inspiration or real content.

'Abstraction' is a term notoriously misused in writings about modern art. What it cannot properly be made to mean is 'non-representational, non-objective art, concerned in no way with nature but only with pure form'. On the contrary, abstract art, properly defined, is 'drawn from' nature, an abstract of nature, and so, though it is, so to speak, at a distance from nature, it always implies it and has reference to it. It could thus be made to apply to all that large field of art which lies between the non-representational and the naturalistic—a field which includes almost all African art. However, it is probably most characteristically applied to a bold, uncompromising stylization, and we shall give here a few examples chosen with this in mind (though there are many others in the book).

Our first example is a large hardwood mask, facing two ways, from the Babembe who live on the Congo shore of northern Lake Tanganyika (Biebuyck collection, 16 *in* without feathers). It represents 'Alunga, the spirit of the bush, and belongs to the men's society; the dancer, his body covered by raphia, sings in a deep guttural voice, accompanied by drummers. Payments given for making such a mask amount to between a third and a half of those given for a wife.

The dance headdresses of the Ham or Jaba and neighbouring pagan tribes of central Nigeria (here seen at the Ham village of Nok in 1949) are advanced examples of abstraction, their derivation from human forms being barely discernible, perhaps because the tribe's position as a pagan enclave in a vast area occupied by Moslems has led them to favour geometrical forms out of prudent deference to iconoclastic Islam. The turreted headdress at left, surmounted by a highly stylized human figure, is that of the Mother Spirit, the mythical ancestress of the tribe, while the other figures are her sons, the male ancestors. The dances are performed by the men's society as an increase rite before the spring sowing of the millet and guineacorn.

A much more readable piece of abstraction is this solid head, painted red with powdered camwood, which was probably made to surmount a post outside a chief's hut among the eastern Bapende on the Kasai River in the Congo. It was collected by Émile Torday for the British Museum in 1907 (12 *in*). The jutting beard is also found on certain helmet masks among this eastern group of the Bapende; but in most cases their masks are almost two-dimensional and are worn in front of the face.

The helmet mask opposite was also collected by Torday for the British Museum (17 *in*), among the Isambo, a subtribe of the Bakuba who live in and around Lusambo on the borders of Basonge and Batetela territory. These two tribes are far more addicted to abstraction than the Bakuba, and this piece was probably made by a Musonge or a Mutetela carver.

It is not clear to us what is represented in this remarkable abstraction, but at the same time it does not appear to be merely a free decorative composition. It suggests that very modern form of sculpture which might be described as 'unworkable machines', but since it was collected by Torday among the Bakuba in 1908 it is less likely to have been suggested by a particularly complicated crankshaft than by, for example, raphia cloths with embroidered edges bunched round the waist of a man in dance dress. The object (British Museum, 11½ in) is an example of a unique form of sculpture practised by the Bakuba: powdered red camwood—used for cosmetic purposes and also as a form of currency by this tribe—was mixed with gum and modelled into elaborate and highly decorated shapes, to be given away to mourners at a funeral as mementoes of the deceased by his heir.

If it were necessary to choose one of the European stylistic labels to characterize the prevailing mode in African sculpture—and it is no part of our intention to suggest that this is either necessary or possible—then the choice would probably have to fall on Expressionism. It is well recognized that the tendencies which the term connotes are as old as art, and a history of art could almost be written in terms of the extent to which they are held in check or given free rein. We shall define African Expressionism not in words but in pictures, and our first is the head of a Basonge wooden fetish (though but little wood is here visible) which must surely have been endowed with great powers of violent action (Musée Royal de l'Afrique Centrale, $14\frac{1}{2}$ *in* from chin to horn tip).

The hypertrophy of the feet of a figure is one of the commonest manifestations of expressionism in Africa, and especially in the Congo. It is often suggested that this symbolizes man's faith in a stable universe and his intimate relation to Mother Earth; but although we may recognize expressionism when we see it, it is less easy to be sure what is being expressed. It is likely that some such symbolism is often present, but since this enlargement of the feet occurs especially on stools and headrests, designed to support a weight, the explanation may sometimes be partly architectonic, and in this case it becomes a moot point whether the symbolism produced the form or the form the symbolism. This beautiful and unique headrest, left, from the Bena Lulua of Kasai (Musée Royal de l'Afrique Centrale, 8 *in*) tempts us to think of a sculptural pun (foot of headrest = foot of man), a form of humour to which we believe that African artists are more inclined than they are given credit for.

This curious adze from the Bawongo, an autonomous Bakuba group to the west of the Kasai (Charles Ratton collection, 13 *in*) is not a true tool but a ceremonial development of a tool for parade purposes, being in fact the badge of a carver. Both the great elongation of the blade issuing from the figure's mouth (which would be useless for carving) and the immense extension of the right arm may be seen as expressions of his artistic powers.

The methods of European caricature may often be paralleled in Africa. According to Professor Biebuyck, who collected it, this small woodcarving used in the *Bwami* society among the Balega (Musée Royal de l'Afrique Centrale, *c* 4 *in*) represents an old man weighed down by the many statues and other initiatory objects given to him as a mark of respect by younger kinsmen whom he has helped through the initiation.

This massive Yoruba carving of a mother with children (Royal Ontario Museum of Archaeology *c* 20 *in*) almost certainly does not represent an earth goddess, or any goddess or spirit, but is a piece of shrine furniture, suitable for the altar of almost any god of the Yoruba pantheon, and representing a nameless devotee who symbolizes the general ideas of increase (which all gods are expected to provide), the honour of maternity, etc.

In the border regions of Eastern Nigeria and the Cameroons are found the well-known mask headdresses covered in animal skin to suggest the appearance of human skin and flesh. Some are naturalistic and even serene in expression; others have wide-open mouths, as though shouting, and exaggerated or distorted features which seem to express excitement and other emotions. Wooden figures from this area are little known and often poorly identified. Figures rarely embody such boldness of form as is found in masks, because the forms of these latter must make their impact while seen in violent motion; but expressionist tendencies are found in the figures too in the Cross River area. This compact and powerful figure, from an unidentified village called Nkim, is probably of Ekoi origin (British Museum, $13\frac{1}{2}$ in).

51

The expressionist mode may sometimes attain its greatest intensity of feeling when subjected to some rigid limitation, such as the strong vertical axis of this notably ghostly figure photographed in 1950 in the Musée de la Vie Indigène at Léopoldville. The style is that of the eastern Bapende on the west bank of the Kasai River, but it is a most unusual piece for this tribe, especially in the fact that it appears to be a true fetish (see page 35), such as are found more usually among the Basonge to the east and the Bakongo near the coast to the west. The (to our eyes) sinister appearance of the fetish is greatly enhanced by the long straight hair and by the twisted antelope horn issuing from the crown of the head. It is about four feet high.

52

An outstanding example of expressiveness achieved through form is offered by this mask ($10\frac{1}{2}$ *in*) from the Dan tribes of the border regions of the Ivory Coast and Liberia. It may well have a strong claim to be the finest of all masks of the Dan group, and is one of many monuments to the flair as a collector of tribal art of its late owner, Sir Jacob Epstein. We should beware once more of assuming that the yearning or even grief which it may seem to convey to a European is the emotion which the artist set out to express; this may well have been of a deeper and less specific character.

The mask styles of the numerous tribes of the Dan–Ngere complex in this border region can be roughly divided between a more refined, classical mode associated chiefly with the Dan group and the much more abstract Ngere mode exemplified on the next page.

By comparison with the restrained Dan form of expressionism the Ngere form is uncompromisingly extrovert and even violent, with tubular or very bulbous eyes and much emphasis on stark geometric forms. This piece (Ratton collection, 12½ *in*) is unusual for being made not of wood, but of basketry covered with clay.

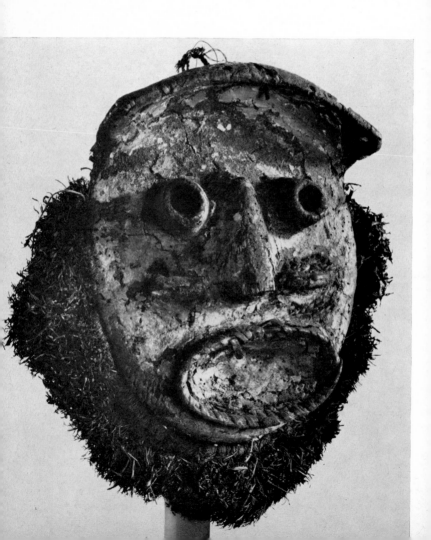

The Ibo of the Onitsha-Awka district of Eastern Nigeria have an important masquerade cult called *mmwo* (ghosts or spirits); besides large and powerful horned masks representing male spirits, they use larger numbers of white-faced, female masks of more gentle appearance. This example (British Museum, 16 *in*) is of the general shape of these female masks, but its component forms are carved with such purposeful crudity and combine to make such a forceful image of violence that it must surely represent a male spirit.

The Grasslands of the Cameroons have produced some of the most powerful of African sculptures in the expressionist mode. There is a vigour and movement in many of them which is sometimes enhanced by imaginative use of space defined by large curved planes, as in this mask from the Bikom tribe (collection of Professor J. R. King, Edinburgh, 17 *in*). Three dogs are seen at the top.

Some of the most striking works in expressionist modes are found among the *makishi* masks of the great Lunda–Bajokwe tribal complex which spans a vast area of Angola, the southern Congo as far east as Lake Tanganyika and Northern Rhodesia in the upper Zambezi valley. This big mask ($16\frac{3}{4}$ *in*), which formed part of the collection of Sir Jacob Epstein, may have come from the Mambunda or Lovale of northern Barotseland on the Zambezi.

Bring me my bow
of burning gold (*Blake*)

This poetic image may help to suggest the deep intensity and pent-up life force of this figure, conceived on a curve such as that of a drawn bow. It is by such means that movement is suggested dynamically in African (and other tribal) art, rather than, as in the naturalistic European tradition, by the representation of arrested movement (*eg* in the Discobolus of Myron), which is essentially static.

This figure of a woman collected by Professor Roy Sieber in 1958 in the Montol village of Baltip in Northern Nigeria was in use for the cure of sickness, a purpose for which the life force, which in African religious belief is the very stuff of nature, is needed in copious supply; its control would be the main function of the figure (Wielgus collection, $15\frac{1}{2}$ *in*).

58

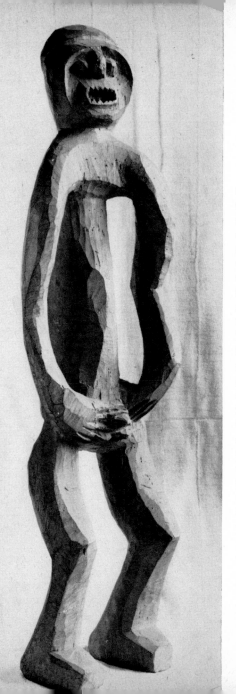

Our final example in this group of sculptures selected to illustrate expressionist tendencies in African art (though these can be discerned also in many other works in this book) is an exceptionally forceful ancestor figure from those masters of expressionism, the Bamileke of the Cameroons Grasslands (British Museum, 37½ *in*). Their forms are freer than those of almost any other tribe, and their works are notable for their disdain of finish. Many a European artist has preferred his sketches to his finished paintings and has resented the necessity of coating them with a saccharine envelope to please the public taste; this is in part what the modern movement was about (though it soon developed its own fashions).

The ancestor cult is intimately connected in African dynamistic belief with the supply of force to the tribe. But we should not jump to any precise interpretation of this figure's posture (at least the citizens of Brussels will not be offended by it).

We have said much of departures from naturalism in African sculpture; let us now for a space consider the occurrence in it of naturalism and naturalistic elements.

The most famous manifestation of naturalism in Africa is the ancient art of Ife, which we suppose to have flourished about the thirteenth century AD. Its origins are a matter of much dispute: is it the antithesis of all other African art, or is it rather one extreme of the vast range of formal experiments produced by African artists?

This remarkable photograph was taken by Mr H. L. Ward Price, District Officer at Ife, in 1931 in the Iwinrin Grove on the outskirts of the town just off the Ibadan road. It shows the principal remains of the nearly life-size terra-cotta figures which must have been a wonderful sight in earlier days. Behind stand Chief Obalara and other priests of the cult of Owinni, an early hero whose shrine is a sanctuary for smallpox sufferers; the idealization of the terra-cottas is evident.

In 1958 a further group of terra-cottas in the same style were excavated, by Mr Frank Willett, in another part of the town, Ita Yemo. An unusual view of the best-known of these (Ife Museum, $9\frac{1}{4}$ *in*) is here included, to draw attention to the interest of these artists in perfection of detail.

Among the Ita Yemo finds of 1957–58 was this bronze staff mount, ornamented with two gagged heads, presumably of sacrificial victims, which carries naturalism further in one respect than any other African work known to us. For reasons which may have something to do with African concepts of time, African artists never seem to represent their subjects as of any particular age. It is impossible to distinguish the carved face of a man from that of a woman, except by the beard, if any, or the coiffure; and a beard is used to indicate manhood rather than old age. With the single exception of this piece (Ife Museum, $3\frac{1}{2}$ in), wrinkles and other ravages of age upon the skin and flesh are absent from African sculpture, almost as though the subjects were represented four-dimensionally, by reference to their whole life rather than to a specific phase of it.

It is uncertain how far Mediterranean influences may have played a part in the extraordinary development of naturalism at Ife. But certainly this was not its first appearance in West Africa, for naturalism was well within the range of the terra-cotta sculptors of the Nok Culture more than a thousand years earlier. In this beautiful head from Wamba in Northern Nigeria (Jos Museum, $5\frac{1}{2}$ in), the artist showed an appreciation of the volumes of the human cranial dome which has been equalled only in one or two of the Ife terra-cottas, and not at all in more recent work. The face too is surprisingly naturalistic, if a little paedomorphic or childlike (apart from the classificatory beard).

64

The naturalism of Ife was transmitted, as we know from traditional evidence and could in any case deduce from stylistic comparison, to Benin, probably about AD 1400. On these pages we illustrate three heads, in terra-cotta and in bronze, of the earliest surviving type in the great corpus of four centuries of art-production found by the British expedition in the palace of the Oba of Benin in March 1897. The terra-cottas appear to have been non-royal equivalents of the bronzes, and to have been made by the bronze-founders for the service of their own ancestor cult and in particular that of Igue'gha, the original master founder from Ife.

The terra-cotta (British Museum, $7\frac{1}{4}$ in) and the two bronzes (British Museum, $8\frac{1}{4}$ in, and Schnell collection, $8\frac{1}{4}$ in) are clearly of one style and period; but it is also evident that a certain amount of individualization was possible, for of all the known early bronze heads (about twenty), only two or three are so similar to each other as to seem to be by one hand, and though the iconography (coiffure, scarification marks, beaded collar) is constant, there are noticeable differences in the different artists' conceptions of the human head. This is evident even from a close look at the two heads here shown, which are among the more similar. Later, such variations were ironed out in a pedestrian conformity.

The same slightly modified naturalism is found in certain royal masks from this early period at Benin. The ivory mask (in Mrs K. Merkel's collection, *c 8 in*) is one of several worn about his person by the Oba during certain ceremonies; the brass one opposite (12 *in*) is part of the regalia of the Ata of Idah, a hundred miles to the north-east from Benin, and may date from about 1515, when the Oba of Benin conquered Idah and put his son on the throne.

Slightly less naturalistic again, but still essentially so, is this little bronze head (Nigerian Museum, 3 *in*), one of two found in a great hoard of finely cast bronze objects dug up at the Ibo village of Igbo-Ukwu, not far from Awka in Eastern Nigeria, in 1939. Excavation by Mr Thurstan Shaw in 1959–60 showed that the finds were part of the grave goods of a buried chief, probably the divine king of the Nri, and suggested that they may have been buried with him a number of centuries ago. Both the divine kingship and the bronzes are strange things to find in Iboland, and may have their origins in the period when the Jukun came down from Kwororofa on the Benue and held sway over a vast area including the Igala and northern Ibo country. The naturalism of this head may possibly be due to Ife–Benin influence by way of Idah, the Igala capital—but this assumes it to be of later date than the Ife style.

For an early example of naturalism of posture (though not of bodily proportion) we return to the Ita Yemo finds at Ife for this bronze couple, apparently an Oni of Ife in full regalia (right) affectionately twining his (presumably boneless) left leg round his consort's right one (Ife Museum, 12 *in*). (The Oni's whole face is lost; the three openings on the buttocks of the figures appear to have had the technical function of permitting the escape of gases from the clay core during casting.)

A smile by no means archaic is worn by this Yoruba boy in European dress carved as the ornamental top to a weaver's heddle pulley (Harold Rome collection, $7\frac{1}{4}$ in). Yoruba wood-carving style is, indeed, founded in naturalism, though often enough departing from it. By comparison with most other tribal styles it may be called humanistic, relying far less than they do on symbolism, representing not gods or spirits but their devotees and other ordinary people. For this reason, and because the practice of traditional art is still alive (if not often vigorous) in many Yoruba villages, this is probably the most favourable ground for a development of the tribal art, for Christian or secular purposes, so that it should remain viable and vigorous even in a largely Westernized society. This is a difficult enough task, but Father Kevin Carroll's work has shown that progress can be made, and it is much to be hoped that many Yoruba will see its value and help to preserve their art in life rather than only in museums.

In very similar vein these pipes for smoking tobacco or more probably *bhang* (Indian hemp) were carved by Bena Kanioka artists of the southern Congo in the form of laughing women, the mouthpiece being in the top of the head (British Museum, 13 and 10 *in*). Though not sculpturally distinguished, they are useful demonstrations of the fact that naturalism of the *genre* type is quite at home in Africa, even in its heart where there was no Western influence.

Beyond the great basins of the Niger and Congo Rivers, sculpture is scarcely found: its main manifestations are among the Makonde of the Tanganyika–Mozambique border region (whose style is basically naturalistic, though often inflating naturalism into caricature), and on the great island of Madagascar, where, however, the culture and perhaps the sculpture is half African, half Indonesian. The most impressive of the island's sculptures are the grave posts, a South-East Asian culture element, though they are often surmounted by figures of a more African character. Of these, the finest known example is this one from Sir Jacob Epstein's collection ($39\frac{3}{4}$ in), a masterpiece of sensitive naturalism fit to stand with the finest sculptures of the mainland.

Around the Congo mouth, a region long subject to European influences, naturalism has been practised so much and so long that it sometimes becomes 'academic'. This 'speaking likeness' of a mother, unclothed but carrying a furled umbrella as a status symbol, and her son (British Museum, 31 *in*) represents life but has little or no sculptural life. We would not dissent from our friend Leon Underwood's verdict on this piece as 'a waxwork'. (The scarification on the mother's breast preserves the textile-derived decorative style of the old Kingdom of Kongo.)

Assorted aspects of naturalism are illustrated in these three works. The first is an excellent example of the small brass figures made by the Fon tribe at Abomey, capital of the Dahomey kingdom; it represents a royal hunter with dane-gun and pointing dog (Margaret Plass collection, 7 *in*). Second is one of the pottery figures (for another see William Fagg, *Nigerian Images*, plate 133) made by the locally famous Goemai woman potter Azume, who seems to have invented this kind of figure early in the century and who died about 1951 (British Museum, 18 *in*). Third is a much weathered bust from one of the wooden figures (apparently representing a chief's wife) which were fixed over the roofs of chiefs' huts among the Eastern or Kasai Bapende (Harold Rome collection, 17½ *in*); a complete and more recent example is illustrated in Elisofon and Fagg, *The Sculpture of Africa*, fig. 254.

74

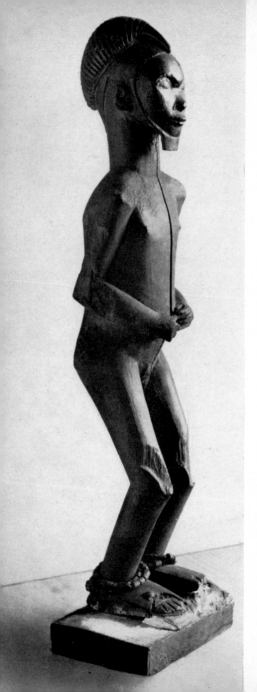

This unidentified male figure from the western Congo (William Fagg collection, 23 *in*) is a good example of the naturalism so frequently found in the area. The only other piece which we know in this style, a bust perhaps cut from such a figure as this, was identified by the late Frans Olbrechts (in *Plastiek van Kongo*, fig. 37) as from the Bakongo, but we are inclined to favour an origin somewhat further inland, since it seems to have affinities with the style of the southern Bambala tribe on the Kwango River, and perhaps also with that of the Bateke somewhat further north. It is remarkable how often African standing figures, even when naturalistically carved, are shown with knees flexed as though in the dance. It may be that the artists had dancing in mind (and much research remains to be done on the relations between dance and sculpture in Africa); but it is also possible that they wished to provide some formal support for the upper masses of the body, and especially the head, which is commonly shown in increased proportion.

76

This Dahomey caryatid (which has been in the British Museum for over seventy-five years, 7 *in*) supports a bowl to hold the palm nuts used in Fa divination (borrowed by the Fon from the Ifa cult of the Yoruba). Its style, more naturalistic than the 'pure' styles of either the Yoruba or the Fon, and also more highly finished, is probably due to Yoruba influence upon a Fon carver.

These two wooden cups for ceremonial drinking of palm wine (British Museum, 7 and 7½ *in*; a front view of the first appears in Elisofon and Fagg, *The Sculpture of Africa,* fig. 264) are from the Bawongo, an autonomous Bakuba group west of the Kasai. Allowing for some stylization of the faces and the tapering proportion of the women's bodies, the postures and also the body cicatrization are remarkably realistic.

The characteristic squatting figure of Bakongo funerary art (see page 25) is here seen carved (2¾ *in* high) on the wooden handle of a chief's flywhisk. Unlike the stone version, this figure is conceived fully in the round and in a pleasingly relaxed position (Ratton collection, Paris).

The Guro of the central Ivory Coast are best known for their masks (page 153), and few figures are known from them. This female figure, from Mr G. W. Elliott's collection (c 14 *in*), is clearly a Guro work, and, apart from some stylization of the facial features, shows considerable attention to anatomical detail, for example in the bones at the base of the neck.

We have perhaps gathered enough examples of various forms of naturalism to show that it is far from alien in the general context of African art. Here and there, as at the Congo mouth, Western ideas have had some influence on it, but for the most part it is clearly indigenous. If the almost mensurational naturalism of ancient Ife art was due in part to ideas brought from the Mediterranean, whether across the Sahara or across Kordofan from the Upper Nile, it seems likely that they fell on fertile soil.

79

From naturalism to surrealism, whose favourite method is the irrational juxtaposition of more or less naturalistic images. Guillaume Apollinaire invented the name but not the fact of surrealism in 1917, for this again is one of the perennial modes of art which has been used, not universally but sporadically, from the earliest times. We here present three surrealist hands. One is a ladle, of unknown but obviously ritual use, which turns into a gnarled human left hand (British Museum, $18\frac{3}{4}$ in), and is from the Bakuba of the Kasai, a tribe of virtuoso carvers. The second is a wooden right hand of astonishing realism (but for the curious addition of an extra joint to each finger) from the Bissagos Islands (British Museum, $12\frac{1}{2}$ in) ; its surrealism resides less in itself than in the manner of its use, since it dangled from the wrist of an elaborately accoutred dancer, as a third hand.

Our third hand underlies a richly scarified head which forms the bowl of a tobacco pipe of the Bena Lulua of southern Kasai (Antwerp Ethnographical Museum, total length 19 *in*). The Bena Lulua carvers were unsurpassed in Africa for their ability to combine beauty of form harmoniously with elaborate decorative enhancement of surfaces. Dr Albert Maesen considers this piece to come from the Bakwa Luntu, a group closely allied in culture to the Bena Lulua proper.

The wooden figure at left is a remarkable surrealist conception, its body being riddled with holes. It was collected among the Balega in the north-east Congo by Professor Biebuyck, a fully paid-up member of the *Bwami* society, and is in his collection at the Musée Royal de l'Afrique Centrale (*c* 10 *in*); it is called *katanda* (a term used for the wild dispersal of red ants when attacked) and symbolizes the disruptive effect of quarrels on the cohesion of the local descent groups and on the harmony of the *Bwami* society.

Another favourite device of European surrealists is the omission of limbs or parts of limbs. Armless figures occur in a number of African tribes, notably among the Ibo of Bende in Eastern Nigeria. Here is a Bajokwe figure from the southern Congo in which the forearms issue directly from the knees; it was photographed in the Musée de la Vie Indigène, Léopoldville, in 1950 (*c* 8 *in*).

Closely allied to surrealism in Europe is the movement or method which has come to be known as Assemblage (variously pronounced as a French or an English word), which itself is a development from collage. It will come as no surprise to readers to learn that this practice too is quite well known and widespread in Africa. This fearsome mask appears to be from the Ibibio of Eastern Nigeria (British Museum, 28 *in*). A face cut from a calabash, with painted leather ears and tubular calabash eyes, is surmounted by an elaborate model hut in which is a monkey skull, while tied up in a bundle on the roof are two human skulls. Presumably such masks, like fetishes, embody the combined life force of their component materials.

Among the Bambara of Mali, the masks of the *Komo* society are assembled from various materials. A wooden mask with forward projecting jaws like a crocodile's is embellished with two pairs of antelope horns, masses of porcupine quills and quantities of gum, blood and other sacrificial material (R. Sieber collection, 20 *in*).

Opposite is an image of exceptional power from the Kran of south-eastern Liberia. The head is modelled from ground-up cement-like earth from termite hills, and into this are inserted boar's tusks, pygmy hippopotamus canines, duiker horns and other animal excrescences; it is topped by a crown of feathers. It was a great oracle fetish and is called *ga-sua* (University Museum, Philadelphia, collected by Mr Allen Davis, 24½ *in*).

The highest flights of assemblage in Africa were probably achieved in the nineteenth century by the Kalabari Ijo of the eastern Niger Delta in the funerary screens (*duen fobara*) of deceased heads of trading houses in the Kalabari towns of Degema, Buguma and Abonnema. These shrines were made for them in their capacity of chiefs in the *Ekine* cult, otherwise known as the *Sekiapu* ('Dancing People') society, and they were represented on them in the headdresses which they were entitled to wear in the *Ekine* plays in honour of the Water Spirits (*owu*), as is seen opposite (Talbot collection, British Museum, 36 *in*).

Almost all African sculptures are monoxyle or carved from single blocks of wood. But the Delta people, in contact with European seamen and traders for centuries, were influenced by the introduction of carpentry to invent these curiously powerful images made up from separately carved heads, limbs and other parts on a framed background of close-set canes.

The *konde* fetishes of the Bakongo of the Congo mouth area are among the most striking products of assemblage. Human and animal figures are often finely carved as receptacles for the insertion of large numbers of nails and other pieces of iron which, together with 'medicine', endow the fetish with its force, as in the two-headed dog above (British Museum, 24½ *in*).

We have so far spoken of African artists mainly in the mass or at least in the plural. Now we should like to put them forward in their individual aspect, for every artist has his own personal style, which we can identify, and is as much of an artistic individualist as his Western counterpart (though seldom or never a romantic rebel). Our first example is a headrest (Ratton collection, $6\frac{1}{2}$ *in*) by a great but anonymous miniaturist of the Baluba Shankadi in the south-east Congo, whom we may call the Master of the Cascade Coiffures; a dozen or more of his carvings are known, all of them brilliant asymmetrical compositions. The supporter in this piece is preparing to smoke *bhang* or Indian hemp from a waterpipe.

On the strength of the magnificent sculpture on the right, ravaged though it is by white ants, we may designate a Master of the Isare Warrior who flourished in the Osi area of north-east Yorubaland about the third quarter of the nineteenth century and whose work dominates even this area of great sculptural vigour. The carving (about 33 *in* high and photographed in 1959) represents a warrior in full panoply carried on the shoulders of a retainer.

Adugbologe, who died about 1945, was the most famous carver of the great Yoruba town of Abeokuta (where his sons Makinde and Salakatu Ayo still carve in his rock-shelter home). The family specializes in masks for the Egungun cult which honours the ancestors, and this one by Adugbologe (Rautenstrauch-Joest Museum, Cologne, $17\frac{1}{4}$ *in*) represents a man with hare's ears (a hare is also represented between the ears and behind the carved tension drum).

Olowe of Ise in southern Ekiti, who died in 1938, was perhaps the best and most original Yoruba carver of this century. On the right is his finest group of statuary, in the palace of the Ogoga of Ikere, now about fifty years old. It represents the Ogoga enthroned in his beaded crown, with his senior wife standing behind him, and flanked by a mounted warrior and by another wife whose back is beautifully decorated. His rather rare works can be recognized instantaneously.

Another great Yoruba carver was Agbonbiofe Adeshina of Efon-Alaye (which was also Olowe's birthplace, whence he later migrated to Ise); he died about 1944 and is chiefly represented by a large series of magnificent houseposts in the palace of the Alaye of Efon, carved about 1916 after the palace had been burnt. This is one of several on the favourite subject of the mounted warrior (*jagunjagun*). The well-rounded masses are typical of the best Yoruba style, of which Efon was one of the great centres, until about 1930 when most of the carvings in the town were taken out and burnt by members of one of the African Christian churches.

92

Agunna of Oke Igbira, near Ikole in Ekiti, flourished during much the same period as Agbonbiofe (a door from his hand was collected by Frobenius in Ado-Ekiti in 1910), but from the point of view of sculptural form he was almost the antithesis of the Efon master. Instead of the usual rounded, almost fleshy volumes which are so characteristic of Yoruba art, Agunna favoured a severe asceticism expressed in angular and rectilinear forms bordering on cubism, as in the head of the rider (and also of the horse) in this fine post in the palace of the Owa of Ilesha (1959). Within the context of Yoruba form, his idiosyncratic style (which influenced two or three lesser artists of the Ikole district) suggests to us a kind of Gothic mode, in which greater intensity of feeling is sought through emphasis on a strong vertical axis.

93

In the next few pages we will examine the incidence elsewhere in Africa of this verticalizing mode—to which we attach the name 'Gothic' only because the Gothic is its best-known European manifestation. Nowhere was it used more effectively or with more intense conviction than in the ancestor figures (*ekpu*) of the Oron clan of Calabar, of which we have already seen an example (page 10; see also page 143). The present example (Jos Museum, *c* 30 *in*) is one of the older, more heavily weathered figures, and may well date back to the first half of the nineteenth century. It also illustrates (like page 89) how excellence of form is not readily destroyed or obscured by natural decay.

94

One of the most interesting yet least-known of African styles is that, or those, of the Bissagos Islands in Portuguese Guinea. These two rare, if not unique, Bijugos figures have the strong vertical axis, associated with a withdrawn, hieratic quality suggestive of some Egyptian art (British Museum, 19½ and 17¼ *in*).

The Dogon tribe of the Bandiagara Escarpment south of Timbuktu in Mali has produced many figures which show a certain affinity with the Oron figures of Calabar (page 94), in spite of the remarkably different environment. This mother-and-child group from the Epstein collection ($39\frac{1}{2}$ *in*) has a subtle asymmetry, which together with the arrangement of the child seems to impart a suggestion of a helical movement around the rigid vertical axis, whose essential stillness and permanence are thus emphasized.

Two more figures of marked vertical form are seen opposite. The first is from the northern Senufo, who are the southern neighbours of the Dogon. It is one of the so-called 'rhythm-pounders' carried by the young men of the *Lo*, or men's society, in a dance in which they all thump their figures periodically and in unison on the ground, holding them from behind by the upper arms. So this figure (Ratton collection, 53 *in*) is designed essentially for an up-and-down movement. Dogon and Senufo both inhabit the dry, sparse savannah-to-sub-desert country of the western Sudan; the western Ijo, on the other hand, who produced the right-hand figure, live in an almost opposite environment: the creeks, mangrove swamps and rain forest of the Niger Delta. This

96

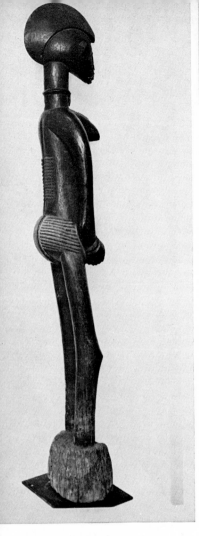

figure (British Museum, 38 *in*) probably represents a 'spirit companion', shown as a chief, to judge by the European hat, of a type which was quickly adopted as a status symbol of chieftainship or civic importance by the Nigerian coastal tribes in the early nineteenth century. These three pieces may stand as a warning against environmental determinism as a method of classifying African sculptures.

This mask, of unusually strong vertical line, is one called *ikpelikpa* from the Igala tribe who inhabit the tract between the lower Benue and lower Niger Rivers. The masks and other carvings of the area around the confluence of these great rivers are still but little known outside Nigeria, but this is undoubtedly an area of the greatest importance in the study of African art history. This mask is in the Nigerian Museum at Lagos (24 *in*).

Our 'Gothic' mode is well illustrated in this notably elongated figure (British Museum, 47 *in*) in the style of the Bambole tribe, south of Stanleyville in the north-east Congo. It is perhaps the largest and certainly one of the most beautiful pieces known in this rare style. These figures are most unusual in having transverse holes pierced at shoulders and buttocks, apparently for suspension against the wall of a hut, and when hung curiously recalls the effect of floating in the air made by Epstein's famous 'Madonna and Child' in lead in Cavendish Square, London. The simplified heart form of the face forms a link in a stylistic chain running from the coastal Fang of the Gaboon through the Bakota and Bakwele to the northern Congo tribes and so to the Bambole and Balega (see page 151).

99

Another ancestor figure from the Dogon of Mali subtly relieves its dominant verticality by means of the transverse forms—beautifully related to each other and to the curve of the trunk—of the breasts, forearms and thighs. This piece (Ratton collection, $23\frac{1}{2}$ *in*) is also of some interest as evidence in a question of Dogon art history. Marcel Griaule recorded a Dogon myth about a legendary people called 'Tellem' who inhabited the escarpment before them and who had migrated to the west. Later, when several caches of old carvings came to light and on to the market from caves in the cliffs of Bandiagara, they were enthusiastically attributed to these Tellem, with the corollary that they were several centuries old. This modern myth still persists in many quarters in spite of the fact that the corpus of 'Tellem' and Dogon sculptures forms an absolutely unbroken continuum both of style and iconography. Few of the 'Tellem' pieces are likely to be much older than 1800. In this piece, we see a 'Tellem' head on a typical Dogon body of the late nineteenth century.

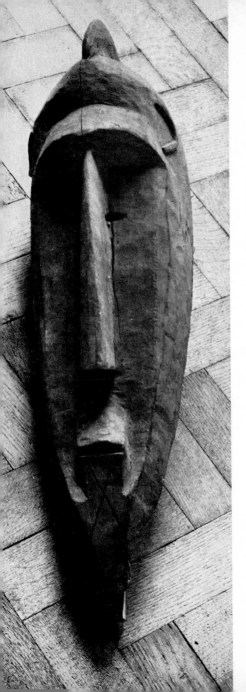

The Edo-speaking tribes to the north of Benin in Nigeria form a universe of art practically unknown to the outside world, but which is extremely rich in new forms such as this remarkable piece of African Gothic, collected from Fuga village in the Kukuruku country by Northcote Thomas early in this century (Cambridge University Museum of Archaeology and Ethnology, $27\frac{1}{2}$ *in*).

There is, of course, a technological explanation for the strong tendency towards a 'Gothic' verticality in African woodcarving. Wood is grained in one direction, and the hardest and closest-grained woods (in which the effects of grain are relatively less important) are but little used by African carvers. Moreover, the soft and medium woods which are principally used often have a marked tendency to crack, and this can be minimized by so designing the work that the centre of the tree is also the centre of the carving. Hence the bias of the woodcarver towards a straight axis, and of the ivory-carvers towards a curved one.

For the reason just stated, it is more difficult to find counterparts in Africa for the Romanesque antithesis of the European Gothic. But horizontalization does occur in some masks or mask head-dresses, notably in this Kuyu helmet mask from the north side of the Congo river (Museum für Völkerkunde, Frankfurt, *c* 16 *in*); and the northern Bambala of the Kwango area of the Congo (or at least one of their carvers) developed a curious specialization of the caryatid figure used as the supporter of a headrest (British Museum, 10¾ *in* wide). The fine palace doors of the north-east Yoruba, such as this one by Arowogun of Osi (British Museum, 114 *in*), do invite comparison with the well-known Romanesque bronze doors of Europe, both in the proportions of their component panels and in the composition of the scenes.

When we look for African parallels to baroque art we naturally turn first to the court arts of the highly developed kingdoms and in particular to Benin City itself. There, the naturalistic Ife-derived art of the early period developed in a baroque direction at the beginning of the middle period, about the third quarter of the sixteenth century. As in Europe, and at much the same time, the increasing, and increasingly secular, pomp and circumstance of court life produced an elaboration of ornament which nevertheless was contained by clear conceptions of form and did not (as later in the rococo) become an end in itself.

In the shield-shaped plaque below (from the Beasley collection, now in the Nigerian Museum, *c* 13 *in*) which is Benin

baroque at its very best, we see either Olokun, god of salt water and wealth, represented as an Oba, or the Oba (perhaps specifically the fourteenth-century Oba Ohen, who becoming paralysed gave out that he had become the sea god) in a divine manifestation, with mudfish instead of legs. The inverted plaque below, though also of a baroque character, is very different from Benin work in style; it is closely related to a pectoral worn by one of the bronze figures at Tada (see Underwood, *Bronzes of Nigeria*, plate 22) and so may be older than the Benin (and European) baroque. It is an outstanding example of the more imaginative, and as yet unlocalized, Lower Niger bronze tradition (British Museum, Plass collections, $6\frac{3}{4}$ *in*).

The remarkable resemblance between this face and those so frequently carved over doorways by Bernini, the great founder of the baroque, is no doubt fortuitous, but within the context of Benin art its balance of form and ornament (in this case of a grotesque character) puts it in the baroque category. It is a hip mask for use with court dress belonging to Chief Ineniguneromwo, head of the brass-casters, and is one of only three known of this design (the others, both in the British Museum, are published in William Fagg, *Nigerian Images*, plate 19, and in Philip Dark, *Benin Art*, plates 81 and 82).

The artist of the fine bronze vase below (Nigerian Museum, *c* 8 *in*) and of its pair in the Museum für Völkerkunde at Berlin (von Luschan, *Altertümer*, figs. 652–4) felt sufficiently at home in the exuberant virtuosity of the Benin baroque to be able to indulge in a sculptor's joke in the two cross-legged figures (one on each side): the finely modelled torso, fully in the round, suddenly turns into a two-dimensional representation at the waist as though flattened by a juggernaut. That this is not a piece of awkward naïveté is shown by the figures and snailshells modelled fully in the round at the waist of the vessel; rather it suggests a measure of intellectual appreciation of the problems of form.

The extreme proliferation of decoration in the bronze *ikegobo* or altar of the hand (as symbol of personal strength or prowess), which is seen below (Jos Museum, diameter *c* 12 *in*), borders on the rococo, but for the firm discipline of the overall design, and must date from the transitional phase between the middle and late periods; it may have been made for an Oba of Benin of the early eighteenth century. It well illustrates the *horror vacui*, or predilection for the covering of all surfaces with decorative enrichment, which is a mark of all Benin court art, at least from the sixteenth century onwards, though it is not noticeable in the tribal art of the Bini.

The baroque finery of Benin court dress is very clearly illustrated in this beautiful bronze figure (Nigerian Museum, *c* 10 *in*); it consists very largely of heavy coral beadwork, but its most striking feature is the extension of the skirt, by means of canes, to rise behind the left arm almost to shoulder height. The date of this piece is something of a mystery: its style shows some affinity with the earliest bronze plaques of the middle period, yet on the sides of the crown are certain ornaments which never occur on the plaques and are held by well-established Benin tradition to have been introduced only by Oba Osemwenede (1816–48). Possibly it is by a less conformist artist who looked for inspiration to the works of the past, which were common enough in the palace.

109

More typical of the figure sculpture of the Benin baroque, yet almost unique in size, is this miniature figure with a hemispherical base (Fuller collection, now in the British Museum, 2¾ *in*), which proves to be a piece in a Benin board game of earlier times. The only other surviving piece (in Mr John Russell's collection) is shown below in position on one of the three surviving bronze boards (Ratton collection, 30 *in*). The game is probably the 'War Game', the former popularity of which in court circles, but not the rules, is recorded in Benin tradition. The two pieces are in precisely the same style as most of the rectangular plaques, so must date from the early seventeenth century.

Even the beginnings of the middle period at Benin show signs of baroque tendencies; but at this stage they are not yet decisive, and a more imaginative development might still have been possible if the fine style represented by this unusual plaque by the Master of the Circled Cross (see William Fagg, *Nigerian Images*, page 34 and plate 20) had not been swamped by the heavier, more pedestrian work of the plaque masters who (presumably) followed him. This shield-shaped plaque, probably meant to be nailed to a door, represents two sixteenth-century Portuguese who, for all we can tell, appear to be catching small Unidentified Flying Objects (collection of M. René Pleven, $13\frac{1}{4}$ *in*).

It is less easy to find analogues to the European baroque when we leave the imperial pomp of Benin, for there are few such cases where a whole culture (that of the court, not of the tribe) can be described as baroque; but among other tribes one can from time to time find baroque-like elements, as in these two ivory armlets collected at Allada in Dahomey in the early seventeenth century by the German merchant Weickmann (Ulm Museum, diameter c. $3\frac{1}{2}$ in). His Dutch partners acquired them in what is now Fon country, but their style is clearly Yoruba; Yoruba artistic influence is still strong among the Fon—to such a point as to cause frequent confusion among ethnologists. Weickmann, like Sir Hans Sloane a little later, was one of those original, if not eccentric, persons who more than three centuries ago were laying the foundations of our present appreciation of the tribal arts.

In what is now known as Guinea (since the term proper to the whole West African coast was appropriated by the newly independent French Guinea), the strength of Islam among many of the Mande-speaking peoples helped to produce among some of those who are still largely pagan some hybrid art forms which suggest those of baroque architecture in Europe. The example here shown (British Museum, $44\frac{1}{2}$ in) is a drum from the southern Baga, a rather little-known group formerly dominated by the Mande-speaking Susu, and is perhaps the finest known example of this style. The drum proper is detachable from its stand at a point just above the frieze of bearded heads. The band of rectilinear ornament below the pegs is derived from the leather-bound Koranic charms universally found among the West African Moslems (and carved in wear round the neck of the female figure); the spacing elements above the head of the main figure are also probably of Moslem origin.

113

For a last example of baroque-like decoration we illustrate another of the Weickmann pieces at Ulm ($22\frac{1}{2}$ in), which is an exceptionally elaborate version of the wooden tray (*pako ifa*) used in Ifa divination by the Yoruba and also (by diffusion from the Yoruba) by the Fon of Dahomey. Three and a half centuries later, it is difficult for us to say whether this piece was carved by a Yoruba, by a Fon or by an artist of some other Slave Coast tribe which used this ancient method of divination, in which palm nuts are thrown and marks made upon the board in accordance with the way they have fallen. Though the design of individual elements is fairly free, the composition as a whole shows marked unity and coherence. Whether the relation between the shapes of the functional blank spaces and the decorated areas owes anything to European influence (which certainly existed on the Coast in those days), it is impossible to say, in the paucity of our information on the other influences operative in West Africa at the time.

When the rococo mode is found in Africa it is almost necessarily due to direct European influence. This is less so at Benin, but as the later bronzes there are almost uniformly unpleasing, we shall seek examples elsewhere, and first of all in Ashanti. Here, then, is an *akrafokonmu* (Leff collection, diameter 6¾ *in*), or gold badge of one of the king's soul-bearers or soul-washers, whose function is to keep his soul free of contamination (the nearest parallel that we can think of in Western society is the tycoon's image-polisher or public relations man). The Ashanti kings, like those of Dahomey, drew heavily on European decorative forms by way of status symbols.

These two extreme examples of derived rococo date from before the Ashanti war of 1873 (British Museum, $6\frac{3}{4}$ and $2\frac{3}{4}$ *in*). In the urn opposite the Ashanti goldsmith has followed European forms very closely, but that the composition is his own is suggested by the tassels on the swathed decoration, which have been freed from gravity and fall upwards. As to the ornament below, it is possible to be familiar with it for years as an exquisite piece of rococo jewellery without noticing that it is a representation of three elephants with birds on their backs; here is a true marriage of European style with African subject matter.

Only among the Ashanti (and to a less extent their relatives the Baule) is gold found in sufficient quantity to influence art forms, but here—if we may argue *ex post facto*—its effect seems to have been devastating, since the well-known dolls, *akua 'ba*, are almost the sole survivors of whatever wood sculpture may once have been practised among them (see page 13).

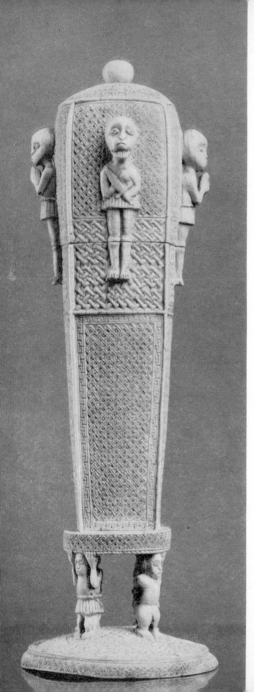

An African, and apparently indigenous, near-equivalent of the luxuriant decoration for its own sake of the European rococo may perhaps be found in the decorative style which appears to have survived from the fifteenth-century Kingdom of Kongo. This style clearly originates in basketry and textile weaving (and still survives in these forms); several large raphia pile cloths with these patterns, collected in the seventeenth century, are in European museums. They were early transferred to solid materials such as ivory and wood, and several old hunting horns in Europe are clearly of this origin. We illustrate a unique ivory box, described as a knife case (Detroit Institute of Arts, *c* 12 *in*), which is the most elaborate example known to us of this Kongo style. As at Benin, the all-over guilloche suggests a *horror vacui*, though in this case it is a natural consequence of its basketry origin. It may be of any age in the sixteenth to eighteenth centuries, and if of the sixteenth should presumably be classed with the Afro-Portuguese ivories made by Sherbro and Bini carvers for Portuguese royalty and nobility.

The treasure of the last king of Dahomey, Gbehanzin, deposed in 1896, was a rich source of African rococo works which were in large part of alien inspiration; in fact, they remind us, except for their greater size, of the latter-day rococo *jeux d'esprit* of Carl Fabergé in the last decades of the Russian Imperial Court. This exquisite silver guinea hen (Verité collection, $13\frac{3}{4}$ *in*), though attributed in one account to the Yacouba of the Ivory Coast, must, we feel, surely have come from the treasure at Abomey with which it is so much in keeping.

An indigenous African rococo which in some ways outdid the European rococo, and seems to have antedated it by a considerable period, is the style of the great bronze or brass hoard unearthed in 1939 and 1960 at the Ibo village of Igbo-Ukwu (see page 68). Many of these finely cast works show an extreme addiction to virtuosity, unparalleled in Africa, which reminds us once more of Fabergé. None of them is quite such a *tour de main* as this extraordinary casting (Nigerian Museum, 13 *in*), represent-

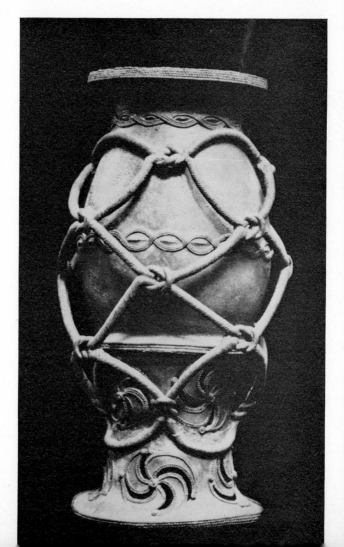

ing a pot resting on an openwork stand, while the whole is encompassed by a rope network. We may admire the skill of the brassfounder without thinking the piece beautiful, and Leon Underwood, who has made a close study of the technique employed in making it, points out to us that (owing to the way in which the wax was assembled) it looks more pleasing if viewed upside down.

One of the most strikingly recurrent modes in the history of human art is the Grotesque, in the sense of the use of plant and animal forms as decorative enhancement for the main subject of a work. In Africa these forms may sometimes occur as a more integral part of the work, as in the widespread types of mask which combine human and animal attributes. An excellent example is this *banda* mask probably from the Baga or the Nalu of Guinea (Zürich University collection, *c* 60 *in*), which represents a being part-human, part-crocodile, part-antelope, besides some other contributing animals. This same form of monster mask occurs all along the coast as far as the Cameroons, where a version of it used to be made at Duala.

The grotesque occurs frequently in the large and assorted group of bronzes which (pending discovery of their place or places of origin) we know as the Lower Niger Bronze Industry. They embody, unlike the Benin bronzes, the most imaginative qualities of African sculpture. Here we have two examples of head-bells or bell-heads, related, no doubt, to certain ritual heads (*omo*) worn by chiefs of the Ijebu Yoruba. Of these two (British Museum, 8 and $5\frac{1}{2}$ *in*), that at the right is from a hoard dug up on the Forcados River in the western Niger Delta, and among other motifs includes one of a decapitated man being pecked by birds; the other is of an as yet unidentified style.

The grotesque is not entirely absent from the court art of Benin City (see, for example, pages 104 and 106), but it is much more characteristic of the group of miscellaneous styles of unidentified origins which it still seems best to group under the name of the Lower Niger Bronze Industry. Some of them have been found in Benin City itself—though certainly not products of the *Iguneromwo* or Oba's brass-casters—and of these probably the most grotesque of all is this head, found by Dr R. E. Bradbury on an obscure shrine in honour of a legendary giant named Enowe (Benin City, *c* 10 *in*). There were some indications that the cult, with this and other bronzes, might have come from the north-east of the Benin Kingdom or beyond. Grotesqueness is, of course, largely a question of subject matter rather than of style, as here in the frog issuing from the mouth, and the snakes issuing from the nostrils and devouring rather simian human figures—images which also have a surrealist aspect.

Whereas on the previous page we showed a basically human head on which animal attributes had been superimposed, we here show another example of the fusion of human and animal in a mask, this time from the Gio of F'eaplay village in eastern Liberia. Most masked dances in Africa may be said to have as a part or aspect of their function the establishing and reinforcing of man's creative unity with nature, expressed in the forms of the masks, in the movements of the dance, and in the music and song which accompany it. It is no doubt the achievement of this unity, this fusion, which brings about the increase of life force to the community.

No part of West Africa offers more favourable ground for the grotesque in art than the Niger Delta, where water spirits play a dominant part in the religion, and are nearly always represented in monstrous animal or animal—human forms. The Abua (a small tribe speaking a semi-Bantu language related to Ibibio) live on its eastern creeks, close to the Kalabari Ijo and the Ekkpahia Ibo. Their masks or headdresses are worn flat on the head, like those of the Ijo, and are made for the *Egbukele* society, which corresponds to the *Ekine* or *Sekiapu* of the Ijo. This example (a composition of cones, spheres and cylinders) has no clear resemblance to any known animal, though the head and ruff have a slight suggestion of the chameleon about them (British Museum, 24 *in*).

Water spirit masks often take fish forms, usually of a monstrous character, as in this many-finned shark, which, like the last, was collected by P. A. Talbot among the Abua (or possibly the Ekkpahia) about the time of the First World War (British Museum, 48 *in*).

Yoruba ivory-carving sometimes takes grotesque forms, especially in the armlets of chiefs. The element of technical virtuosity may be present, too, as in this fine example in the style of Owo, which has two interlocking cylinders carved in the manner of Chinese boxes from a single block (British Museum, $6\frac{3}{4}$ *in*). Besides a considerable profusion of human and animal forms, there is the widespread Abraxas-like figure which has mudfish for legs. We have seen two striking examples of this conception on pages 104 and 105, and it appears to be a symbol of great importance in Yoruba and Benin iconography. Similar forms are of course well known in the Mediterranean, from Gnostic times to the charms still used in the Naples area, though in these the legs are replaced rather by snakes; a Nigerian version with snakes occurs on an openwork bronze armlet belonging to the Aku of Wukari, the king of the Jukun tribe on the middle Benue. Snake cults, usually associated with the grotesque in art, are both common and important along the West African coast, especially in Dahomey; we know of a metal figure purporting to be an ancient North Syrian mother goddess in the Brooklyn Museum, which we are firmly convinced (whatever metallurgical opinion may say) can be none other than a fine Dahomean work of the nineteenth century representing a snake priestess, her arms and body beautifully entwined with a pair of snakes.

The grotesque elements in many of the Kalabari Ijo masks are in the form of relief decoration, consisting for example of tortoises (symbols of wisdom) or coiled snakes, as in this mask called *igbo*, which is said to be a great womanizer (British Museum, $15\frac{1}{4}$ *in*). Python cults are numerous and important in the Delta, and much rarer elsewhere in Nigeria, so that what we may recognize formally as a grotesque mode, or grotesque elements, in the art are no mere fashion nor yet surrealist fantasies, but are a functional outgrowth and manifestation of religious belief. We must also beware of thinking of the simplifications of Ijo art as necessarily fearsome in intention. Some cults do, or did, set out to inspire fear as well as awe, but the same rather rigid style of art is used for comic purposes and for cults which are essentially gentle and beneficent; one of the most fearsome-looking images known to us represents a man's guardian spirit.

The python cults of the Delta tribes—in which large live pythons are often kept in a more or less domesticated state, their food provided by the priests and devotees—must have had some influence upon imperial Benin, for although there does not seem to be any evidence for python cults there, enormous bronze pythons, cast in sections and forty feet long, according to some reports, were mounted on shingled turrets over the gates of the Oba's palace at least as early as the early seventeenth century (since they are illustrated on some of the plaques). The head shown may be of the seventeenth century (University Museum, Philadelphia, $13\frac{1}{2}$ in). Here the power symbolism of the python cults, but not their religious content, appears to have been taken over by the Obas for their own material and political purposes. Once again therefore we find that the European labels which we have been trying out on African art can be applied with more real meaning in the special conditions of the Benin Kingdom than elsewhere in Africa.

The somewhat effete art of the last European *fin de siècle* may seem rather unlikely to have a parallel in Africa, but Art Nouveau, so far from being new, is another recurrent mode in man's arts, and its forms are by no means tied to decadence in the body politic. This fine ivory box from Benin (Nigerian Museum, *c* 6 *in*), with its writhing animal and plant forms, was almost certainly carved there (independently, of course) during Mucha's heyday in Paris in the 1890s.

The bronze tube of uncertain use which is seen at left above belongs to the Lower Niger Bronze Industry and dates very probably from the seventeenth century. Yet its sinuous lizard and snake forms against an open field relieved by small, irregularly spaced knot-like motifs might have strayed from the cover of the *Studio* or the *Yellow Book.* The brass snufftaker (worn elegantly on the little finger to take snuff from the round top) is from the Tiv of Northern Nigeria—among the least open to alien influence of all West African tribes—and was probably cast early this century; we may be sure that the Art Nouveau birds are a Tiv creation (University Museum, Philadelphia, $15\frac{1}{4}$ *in*; British Museum, $6\frac{1}{4}$ *in*).

In all the foregoing, it has by no means been our hope to start a fashion for studying African sculpture under European artistic categories or '-isms'. On the contrary, we think that even when formal correspondences are found, these seldom extend to a similarity of function or real content. Our experiment has been designed to squeeze from these comparisons such value as we could find in them, and so to show how far the European categories are and are not applicable in Africa. If such equations have little permanent validity, we have, we feel, shown them to have a certain heuristic value, that is, they have helped us, and we hope also the reader, to form our own views about form in African art. Provided that they are used critically, they furnish one means of clearing our minds of cant, of our own preconceptions, before seeking to discover the categories inherent in the sculptures themselves, and in what we know of their African context.

In the last pages of this book we shall discard such alien distractions and consider a further selection of African works as far as possible on their own merits and in their own terms.

The mask illustrated opposite ($13\frac{1}{2}$ *in*) we feel to be among the most expressive of African sculptures, even if it suggests a little too easily to Western eyes a melancholy which may have been far from the carver's intention. It is from the magnificent collection of our greatly lamented friend Tristan Tzara, one of the founders of Dadaism who at the same time had the deepest respect and understanding for the traditional art and artists of Africa. We cannot offer any documentation about it, since its origin has remained a puzzle for many years. An old label inside it attributes it to the Susu (of 'Senegal'), but we know of no stylistic corroboration for this and think it unlikely, although anything is possible in the inadequately studied areas of Guinea, Sierra Leone and Liberia. To us it seems to have more affinity with the rare masks from various areas of eastern Africa, and more especially with those of the Makonde–Makua–Mawia group of tribes in the Tanganyika–Mozambique border area.

These two small masks from the Dan complex of tribes in the Liberia–Ivory Coast border area (British Museum, 6 and $5\frac{3}{4}$ *in*) are included not for exceptional merit, although they are good ones, but because they are the earliest examples known to us, having been acquired by the British Museum in 1868; they came to light some years ago in the North American reserve collections (doubtless because of a piece of wampum-like beadwork which is attached, with a monkey skin, to one of them).

134

Figure sculpture from the north-east corner of the Congo is both rare and simple, and this woodcarving (American Museum of Natural History, 24 *in*) is the most elaborate known to us. It must probably have been made for a cult among the Mangbetu, who make carvings not only for themselves but also for the Azande and some smaller tribes of the area.

Of all the styles of African sculpture, it is that of the Baule of the Ivory Coast which is most frequently adopted as their first favourite by those embarking on the formation of an African collection. This appears to be because of the ingratiating quality of the great majority of Baule pieces, a superficial suavity which is often accompanied by a lack of firmness of structural form. In fact, the Baule were remarkably quick to adapt themselves in a very subtle way to the good opinions which French administrators and other visitors formed of their work, and not only produced large quantities of carvings intended for export but used this subtly Frenchified, rather saccharine style for works for their own use. Moreover, Himmelheber avers that many of their figures have no other function but that of recording the beauty of pretty girls—a highly unusual practice in Africa.

But there are outstanding exceptions which place the Baule at their best in the front rank of sculptors, and this figure (Ratton collection, 16 *in*) is one of the finest of them.

This fine old figure (Ratton collection, 19$\frac{1}{4}$ in) has an originality of form which makes it somewhat difficult to identify exactly. It is attributed to the Bakongo, and the attribution is probably correct, the most likely place of origin being towards the north of the Bakongo territory and somewhat inland, perhaps on the borders of the numerous small tribes, including the Balali, who practise art styles of the Balumbo type. The conceptualization of form is of a very African character whose quality it would be very difficult to analyse in words. The spaces between arms and body have a sculptured quality as well as the forms themselves.

An important form of African sculpture which has inevitably received too little attention in the Western world—because it cannot be collected, or indeed moved, without falling to pieces—is the mud sculpture which is found especially among the Bini and the Ibo, but also among other peoples from Togoland to the Cross River. Some of the older groups, dating from early this century, have excellent sculptural qualities, but more recent ones show marked formal degeneration, as is well demonstrated in Ulli Beier's recent book, *African Mud Sculpture*. This example was photographed in 1958 at the Bini village of Ugboko about thirty miles south-east of Benin City, and is the shrine of a river goddess; the figures are life-size and the smallest, at the back, represents Osanobua, the supreme god, whose figure is usually of later manufacture, showing the influence of the Benin court style in the coral bead ornaments.

Between Benin and the Niger live certain western Ibo groups, and among them the Kwale Ibo formerly practised a form of pottery sculpture of considerable merit, if not of great material strength. Fragments of this style can still be found in the village of Osisa, but the existing complete examples seem to have come to England in the eighteen-eighties. They were made for the cult of the Yam Spirit, Ifijioku, and whereas most of them are freestanding groups (representing the family making sacrifices to the spirit), they include this pot with smaller figures under the lip (British Museum, $14\frac{1}{2}$ *in*). This is among the most humanistic (though not naturalistic) of African arts.

If African ancestor figures in their innumerable styles have a quality in common, it is surely that of *gravitas*, expressing the deep reverence (tempered with familiarity) in which the deceased elders of the tribe are held. They have been promoted by death to a higher status, in which they perform an indispensable function as intermediary channels of life force for the tribe; at the same time they are in a reciprocal relationship with their living descendants, on whose survival as a line and unbroken service they are dependent for their own wellbeing in the after life. This example (Royal Scottish Museum, 31 *in*) is from the Batabwa, a Baluba or Baluba-ized tribe at the south end of Lake Tanganyika.

Yoruba sculptural design is seen at its finest in this figure (about 30 *in*) photographed in the shrine of Oyalakun at Ilobu in central Yorubaland in 1958. An effect of great nobility has been achieved by purely sculptural means, the slender, curved forms of chin, breast, forearm, thigh and feet responding to each other like the oscillations of a seismograph or the controlled eccentricity of the master drummer's beat. The static pose and the dynamic rhythm are reconciled, and to us, though it is seated, it even suggests a sculptural translation of the dance. It is a kind of synthesis of the arts.

Ulli Beier, in his *The Story of Sacred Wood Carvings in One Small Yoruba Town*, made Ilobu famous for the devotion with which the people preserved their fine old carvings (many of them, as this, about a century old) from the ravages of climate and insects; but in the end they were defeated by human termites, and Beier saw his tribute used as a thieves' handbook. During 1961 and 1962 a third of their carvings, including this very piece, were stolen to feed the international art market.

The Benin baroque, which we have considered at some length on pages 104–111, finds a rustic echo in this charming bronze figure of a chief (Vincent Price collection, $18\frac{1}{4}$ in) ; it belongs to the Udo style—so named because it is clearly separate from the Benin court style (though drawing its iconography from it), and several pieces in the style are known to have been in the possession of the chiefs of Udo, a town some twenty miles west of Benin. This is one of the very few cases in Africa in which it would not be wholly inappropriate to use the term 'folk art', since it is a popularization of an aristocratic art. Apart from such rare cases, African society is not stratified in the manner characteristic of Western societies, in which the art of the aristocratic or the wealthy level filters down after a period and is reinterpreted and simplified by the 'folk'.

142

Our observations on the *gravitas* of ancestor figures (page 140) apply with especial force to this *ekpu* figure from Oron—one of a number of such figures in the Oron Museum near Calabar (on loan from the families which still own them) which were stolen in 1958 and have been traced in various parts of the world; this one, the finest of the stolen group, was, happily, recovered in Europe. Once we have cleared our minds of the image of Colonel Blimp and the comical associations of the billycock hat (here the mark of a chief), we can begin to see how the forms of this figure both express and inspire respect for the ancestor. Let us note, by the way, that ancestor figures are seldom if ever 'portraits' in any sense current in Europe or America. A bearded statue does not mean that the ancestor had a beard, only that he was a man.

143

The Janus image—the double figure facing both ways, commonly male and female—is a recurrent theme in most parts of the sculpture-producing area of Africa, and reflects the constant emphasis on dualism and reciprocity in African thought and life. The example at left below is a fine old ivory, stained a deep reddish black, collected from the Balega before 1925, and like all their art undoubtedly made for the *Bwami* society (British Museum, $6\frac{1}{4}$ in). The ivory figure below right (Professor Biebuyck's collection, c $4\frac{1}{2}$ in) is of a type called *igenga*, held individually as emblems and initiatory objects by members of the highest grade of the *Bwami*. The peculiar form of the lower torso appears to have been designed by the sculptor as a kind of response to the form of the head.

That the Fang, Pangwe or Pahouin of the Gaboon were among the greatest African masters of form can be seen, for example, from Elisofon and Fagg, *The Sculpture of Africa*, figs. 164–175. We illustrate a smaller carving (Ratton collection, 9 *in*) which exhibits the same plastic qualities and well suggests the sensuous humanism expressed by these artists in their exceptional attention to the fleshy parts of the body and to a skin beautiful in itself and needing no decorative enhancement. It may seem strange, in face of the charm of such works, to remember that the Fang were among the fiercest warriors and cannibals in Africa, but this is a typically African paradox, and hardly more surprising than the occurrence of the idealized naturalism of the classical style of Ife in a town which, even in early times, must have presented—to the hygienically conditioned Western eye—an aspect of squalor and dilapidation comparable to what we see there today. (Where in the world can a culture be found which is in all respects beautiful?)

Two problematical masks provide us with an opportunity, un-trammelled by documentation, to notice in their contrast the emphasis on life in African masks. The one at left (Brooklyn Museum, $12\frac{3}{4}$ *in*), with its blank Egyptian stare, imparts, perhaps intentionally, an absence of feeling. It is one of several unidentified masks in the same style which give an impression of coming from the north-east Congo or the region of the Great Lakes; but Professor Biebuyck's non-recognition is decisive against a Balega origin. The brass mask at right (British Museum, from the Epstein collection, $6\frac{1}{4}$ *in*), on the other hand, seems instinct with eager life, expressionistically projected in the popping eyes and flaring nostrils. At first sight these features suggest the brass-casting style of Bamum and Bamenda in the Cameroons Grasslands; but iconographic connections with Benin and probable affiliation with the Lower Niger Bronze Industry are indicated by the Bini tribal marks on the forehead, the iron inlay of the eye pupils and the slits beneath the eyes—unless indeed this is a creative re-interpretation by a Bamenda artist of a Benin mask shown to him.

146

This cone head (British Museum, $21\frac{3}{4}$ in), which reminds us of the bronze bell-heads of the Lower Niger (pages 122 and 123) and is also similar to certain brass-plated headdresses in the south-east Yoruba district of Okitipupa, is one of a group of headdress masks collected by the Benin Expedition of 1897 at Ughoton, the river port of Benin. They belonged to the cult of Igbile, a river spirit, who shares a small shrine with Olokun, the god of salt water; after their removal, somewhat crude replacements were made by the devotees, and these are still in use. This is a case of trans-tribal diffusion, for the Bini of Ughoton obtained the cult and the mask style from the Ilaje, the south-easternmost group of the Yoruba, who in turn learned the style from the western Ijo. The schematic nose and mouth are especially typical of Ijo style, but the drooping eyes seem to introduce a more sensitive note.

Our final pages will be devoted to horns and related forms expressive of growth, because this is one kind of sculptural form which is very frequently found in African and other tribal art, whereas in the post-tribal art of civilizations it is conspicuously absent.

Of these two remarkably similar images associated with kingship, that seen above is a ritual palm-wine cup of a type reserved for the use of kings of the Bakuba of the Kasai (British Museum, 11 *in*). The other (17 *in*), opposite, is one of three such heads, called *osamasinmi*, on the ancestor altar of a chief of the royal lineage at Owo in eastern Yorubaland, which are used mainly in the ceremony of the cutting of the first yams; thus they are part of an increase cult. In each case the artist has conceived the idea of setting off the great sweep of the ram horns with a triangular pointed form (the ear) centrally placed in the space which they enclose.

From a little-known south-eastern subtribe of the Senufo we illustrate two aspects of growth curves. The mask above left (British
Museum, 15¾ *in*), collected near Jimini just inside Ghana in
1889, is conceived mainly in two dimensions but has highly
formalized horns (one broken off) as the main motif of its super-
structure. The other (Ratton collection, 14 *in*) is itself conceived
as a kind of horn or shell form which is accentuated by the en-
graved lines, approximating to exponential curves, on the coiffure.
Masks in this style are still in use among the Ligbe.

This Balega mask (Biebuyck collection, *c* 6 *in*), called *lukwakongo* and used in initiatory ceremonies leading to the second highest grade of the *Bwami* society, is related to the ancestor cult but does not represent a particular spirit; during initiations it may be carried in the hand, laid on the ground, attached to a fence or fixed to the cheeks or the head. Formally, it is a remarkably clear example of a widely recurrent form in tribal art: it may be compared to an egg from which two intersecting slices have been removed, these slices approximating to exponentially curved planes. The result, seen from the front, is a 'heart-shaped face'—a concept which Dr Douglas Fraser has recently, in his *Primitive Art*, traced in many places and adduced as evidence of diffusion from tribe to tribe over a vast area. We, on the other hand, would interpret it as the natural consequence of the use of growth curves in this way, in presumed association with beliefs about the increase of life force which are common to all tribal peoples.

African religion is manifested largely in the form of increase cults, that is, cults devoted to the increase of the life force available to the tribe, the community and the individual; the belief underlying them is that all things consist of energy or force. Artists are necessarily influenced by these beliefs, and if we find one kind of form (which is peculiar to tribal art) to be especially favoured by them, and notably in cults demonstrably concerned with increase, such as the *osamasinmi* at Owo (page 148), then it is natural for us to surmise that the form is intended to express or symbolize some aspect of the concept of increase.

Excellent examples are the animal masks used in agrarian ceremonies in which the mythical origins of agriculture are re-enacted. In the western Sudan and the Guinea Coast, the antelope is a favourite subject, as in this example from the Bambara (Gernsheim collection, *c 22 in*), in which the horn form is reflected in the ears, the flaring mouth and even the tapering, protuberant eyes.

The same intention receives a somewhat different sculptural expression in the *zamle* masks of the Guro of the Ivory Coast (British Museum, 19½ *in*), but here again the exponential curve of growth in the antelope horns seems to run through to condition the whole form of the sculpture.

For most of us, the exponential principle, if we are aware of it at all, is just an abstruse mathematical concept. Yet the importance which the tribal Africans seem instinctively to attach to the forms which embody it was at least matched by the importance which it assumed for us on 2 December 1942, in Chicago, when Enrico Fermi used the words 'The curve is exponential' to mark the first nuclear chain reaction, which made possible the first atomic explosion. The same mathematical concept, which is that of geometrical progression, is implicit in the now fashionable figurative use of the term 'explosion', as in 'the population explosion'. Tribal peoples know nothing of these concepts, yet their idea of the nature of things seems to have been based from time immemorial on this same principle of increase.

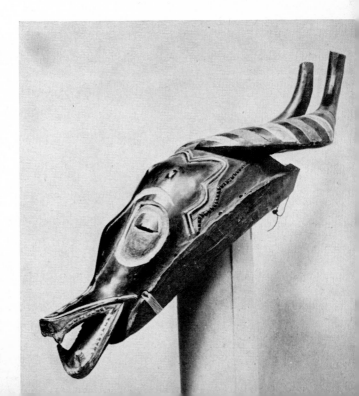

This ganglion of growth curves from the Ibo of Eastern Nigeria (British Museum, 9 *in*) is an *ikenga*, the altar of a man's own right hand (or forearm), by which is meant that aspect of his life force which enables him to meet and overcome the challenges and vicissitudes of life. Before embarking on a difficult or dubious enterprise, the owner would offer kola nuts before the *ikenga*, to fortify his force and to give himself confidence in success. Some *ikenga* are very elaborate, but the only indispensable component is a pair of carved horns—here represented by the two processes of square section at the top of the carving.

Though we have selected horns for special emphasis in these pages, the same principle is evident in the offering of giant snail shells to Obatala, the Yoruba god of creation and growth, and in the frequent use of elephant, hippopotamus and warthog tusks, of bird beaks and claws, and even of human fingernails.

But the influence of these curves seems to go far beyond their direct representation in art, and many sculptures will be found in this book whose forms reflect them in subtle ways. One such (Chaim Gross collection, 19 *in*) we illustrate on this page. It is a wooden figure, probably of a male ancestor, from the northern tribes of the Congo, and is one of the finest carvings known from that region so sparse in population and in art.

These two old ancestor memorials in the form of antelope heads
in the palace of the Onogie of the Ishan town of Ewohimi, north-
west of Benin, illustrate two points very well : one is the striking
difference in artistic effect between a merely average or mediocre
work (behind) and a masterpiece of beautiful form such as the
one in the foreground ; the other (which we have already made
by implication on pages 75 and 89 and more explicitly on page
94) is the near-indestructibility of formal beauty under the severe
attrition of the tropical climate and the white ant, which impartially
erode wooden surfaces, yet allow fineness of proportion to survive until the whole work is reduced to dust. But above all this
masterly piece illustrates the sculptural conception of a whole
head in terms of horn form.

An extreme development of the horn concept is seen in this rare bull mask (British Museum, $50\frac{1}{2}$ *in* wide), with separately carved horns, from the Bissagos Islands of Portuguese Guinea, one of the backwaters of West Africa where fruitful research in tribal art may still be possible.

But perhaps the most powerful image of force and its increase in African art is the *Nimba* mask of the Baga of Guinea. Our last example (page 158) (British Museum, length of head $22\frac{3}{4}$ *in*) is among the oldest and finest known, and well displays the massive cantilevered head (the whole weighs 80 pounds), expanded or projected forward along exponential lines. Nimba is the spirit or goddess of increase among the Baga, and the therapeutic effect of the appearance from the bush of her great image with its sculptured promise of plenty can be easily imagined; by its side the devitalized European symbol of the cornucopia seems trivial and meaningless.

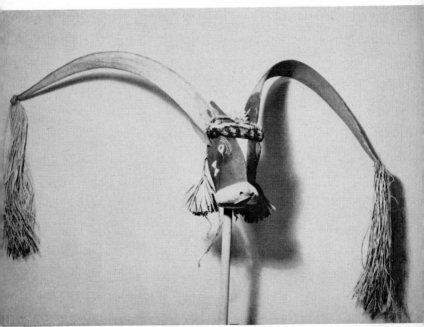

Leon Underwood has pointed out that the great technological advances in the history of mankind have always been followed by equally great developments in art. It may be that when the implications for man's life of the technological changes inspired by mathematical physics in our time are more fully understood, some new movement in art—let us say Exponentialism—will arise to do justice to them. If so, it seems likely that the new ground will be found to have been reconnoitred long before by the intuitive artists of the tribal world.

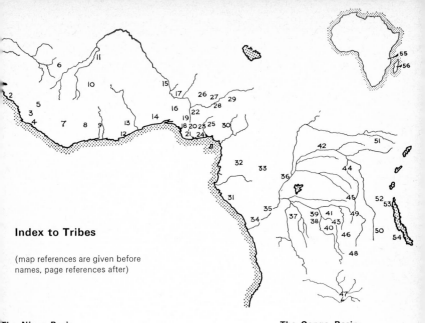

Index to Tribes

(map references are given before
names, page references after)

The Niger Basin and Guinea Coast

21 Abua 125–6
13 Ashanti 13, 29, 39, 115–17
2 Baga 113, 121, 157–8
6 Bambara 84, 152
30 Bamileke 59
30 Bamum 146
15 Bariba 26
9 Baule 117, 136
18 Benin 64–7, 104–12, 118, 122–3, 126, 129–30, 138, 142, 146
30 Bikom 56
18 Bini 108, 118, 138, 142, 147
1 Bissagos Islands 80, 95, 157
29 Chamba 16–17
7 Dan 53–4, 134
11 Dogon 96–7, 100
25 Ekoi 18–19, 51
16 Esie 24
12 Fanti 39
14 Fon 74, 77, 112, 114, 119, 126
7 Gio 124
27 Goemai 74
8 Guro 79, 153
26 Ham (Jaba) 43
24 Ibibio 10, 83
23 Ibo, 30, 41, 55, 68, 82, 120, 138–9, 154
16 Ife 9, 18, 20, 60–3, 65, 68–9, 79, 145

22 Igala 66, 68, 98
23 Igbo 68, 120–1
21 Ijo 34–5, 86–7, 96–7, 125–6, 128, 147
19 Ishan 156
18 Isoko 33–4
28 Jukun 68, 126
5 Kissi 18, 20–2
7 Kran 84–5
19 Kukuruku 101
20 Lower Niger 105, 122–3, 131, 146–7
3 Mende 22, 31
27 Montol 33, 58
2 Nalu 121
7 Ngere 53–4
26 Nok 8–9, 32–3, 63
17 Nupe 12, 24
24 Oron 10, 94, 96–7, 143
10 Senufo 17, 96–7, 150
4 Sherbro 22–3, 118
4 Temne 22, 31
28 Tiv 131
18 Urhobo 34
16 Yoruba 23–4, 26–8, 50, 70, 77, 88–93, 102–3, 112, 114, 122, 126–7, 141, 147–9, 154

The Congo Basin and East Africa

53 Babembe 42–3
40 Bajokwe 57, 82
34 Bakongo 25, 52, 73, 76, 78, 87, 118, 137
33 Bakota 36, 99
41 Bakuba 14–15, 44–6, 78, 80, 148
52 Balega 37–8, 50, 82, 99, 144, 151
50 Baluba 14, 88, 140
31 Balumbo 137
37 Bambala 76, 102
44 Bambole 99
38 Bapende 44, 52, 74–5
49 Basonge 35, 44–5, 47
54 Batabwa 140
35 Bateke 40, 76
45 Batetela 40, 44–5
39 Bawongo 49, 78
46 Bena Kanioka 71
43 Bena Lulua 48–9, 81
32 Fang 11, 99, 145
36 Kuyu 102
48 Lunda 57
56 Madagascar 72
55 Makonde 23, 72, 132–3
47 Mambunda 57
51 Mangbetu 135
42 Northern Congo tribes 155

Index of topics

Abstraction 42–6
Art Nouveau 130–1
Assemblage 83–7
Baroque 104–14
Bernini, Gianlorenzo 106
Brancusi, Constantin 10, 14–15
Cézanne, Paul 8–9, 12, 32, 125
Cubism 11, 32–41, 93
Epstein, Sir Jacob 53, 57, 72, 96, 99, 146
Exponential curve 148–58
Expressionism 47–59, 146
Fabergé, Carl 119–20
Folk art 142
Gothic 93–101
Grotesque 101, 121–9

Individualism 74, 88–93, 102–3, 111
Life force 26, 34–5, 43, 50, 58–9, 83, 87, 124, 140, 148–58
Lipchitz, Jacques 29
Matisse, Henri 31
Metal sculpture 26–9, 62, 65, 67–9, 74, 104–11, 115–17, 119–20, 122–3, 129, 131, 142, 146
Moore, Henry 29–30
Mucha, Alphonse 130
Naturalism 8–9, 42, 60–80
Picasso, Pablo 36
Rococo 104, 115–21
Romanesque 102–3
Stonecarving 18–25
Surrealism 80–3, 123

Bibliography

Beier, Ulli, *African Mud Sculpture,* Cambridge 1963
Beier, Ulli, *The Story of Sacred Wood Carvings in One Small Yoruba Town,* Lagos 1957
Dark, Philip, *Benin Art,* London 1960
Elisofon, Eliot, and William Fagg, *The Sculpture of Africa,* London and New York 1958
Fagg, William, *Nigerian Images,* London and New York 1963
Fraser, Douglas, *Primitive Art,* London and New York 1962 (a strongly diffusionist interpretation)
Leuzinger, Elsy, *Africa: The Art of the Negro Peoples,* London 1960
Luschan, F. von, *Altertümer von Benin,* 3 vols., Berlin 1919
Paulme, Denise, *African Sculpture,* London 1962
Sydow, Eckart von, *Afrikanische Plastik,* Berlin 1954
Trowell, Margaret, *Classical African Sculpture,* London 1954
Underwood, Leon, *Figures in Wood of West Africa,* new edition, London 1964
Underwood, Leon, *Masks of West Africa,* new edition, London 1964
Underwood, Leon, *Bronzes of West Africa,* London 1949